Beautiful

Beautiful

Jaiya John

Soul Water Rising

Silver Spring, Maryland

Beautiful

Printed in the United States of America

Soul Water Rising
Silver Spring, Maryland
http://www.soulwater.org

Library of Congress Control Number: 2008901253
ISBN 978-0-9713308-3-2

FIRST SOUL WATER RISING EDITION: 2008

Poetry / Child & Youth Development

Editorial Team:
Jacqueline V. Richmond
Charlene R. Maxwell
Kent W. Mortensen

Cover design: R. Eric Stone

for our young melodies
yearning to become eternal song

AUTHOR'S NOTE

This poetry is a continuous river of vibrant tears, washing over life's sediment to reveal the shimmering beauty of our uprooted young. Some beauty is hidden beneath youthful blemish. Some beauty stands clear before us. Our challenge is to *see* this radiance. Our young are purpose-full. Beautiful is their *name*.

Beautiful is a poetic companion to *Reflection Pond*. Like *Reflection Pond*, *Beautiful* brings us nearer to youth who have been separated from their original families. Here, young voices encountered in my life's work are rendered in fictional poetry inspired by their sheer human luminosity. I wrote these poems for adults, intending to transmit the honest, unobstructed spirit of children.

Our young are often burdened with categories and labels we assign them. So too is poetry. For this reason, I have allowed these poems to range free, without titles, categories, or sections. Please discover them in your own personal way.

I wrote many of these poems as part of my oral presentations through the years—they are longer and contain rhythm, rhyme, and language designed for narrative messaging and dramatic effect. Such *performance poems* were intended for audiences who were without the advantage of digesting words from the page at their own pace. Other poems in *Beautiful* are more contemplative, concise.

Some poetry is best eaten raw, for the listening soul. Some is best served cooked, for the reader apt to linger on the verbal imagery. *Beautiful* contains a gumbo of such poetic types, all leading to a central truth: Childhood separation reveals our human vulnerability and our human majesty.

She on this day
valedictorian
worthy speaker
rises and steps poised
to the podium

no notes

only a long rehearsed
expression of yearning
for people not present in flesh
a circle of intimacy
she has not seen
in 36 seasons on earth:

Good morning ladies and gentlemen
on this bright and honorable morning
I would like to ask you to excuse me
as I first address some people
who are not able to be here
with us

I am hopeful that you
will take my message to them
as a message to all . . .

clearing the nerves from
her throat and shooing
the butterflies from her stomach
she begins:

To my dear family. . .

on this my graduation day
I want to let you know
how much you have meant to me
even though I have not seen you
in nine years

memories of you are the
sweet blood that runs through
my happiness

the nectar that makes
possible my sorrow

I have furrows
in my character
that your investment entrenched
in plentiful rows

my melancholy now
speaks of a great joy then

for achievement is what remains
after easy things are boiled away

the scent of you opens
the blossom of my heart

dreams of you bring me
back to the shores
of my belonging
sturdy me once more
for my long swim
across this lake of life

stories we shared
now gone to dust
became seed and sprouted
into morals and values
that carry me

our love cannot be eclipsed
by time or distance
cannot be eroded
by tears or tragedy
cannot be placated
so easily as to say
we were family once

nothing is enough
short of saying
we are family still

together we cross
this graduation stage

together our spirits
matriculate through
seasons of living
ascend ladders of purpose
to reach a mystical lake
where only those who
have been loved may bow
and drink a water of
abundance without end.

Ease me
I am that place
where river meets rock
and becomes white water
I am that place of
transformation and foam
I need a tide pool
I need a home

full moon preens
to its own beauty
basking on mirror surface
of placid waters

the child I am is envy swollen
I cast a stone and break
that reflection with ripples
silent and hurried
like the desires
wet and unwelcome
that litter my shore.

An adolescent ponders belongingness:

I wish I was the river

now I am the river stone
cold water diamond clear
rushes over me

life flows past
drowning me in its eternity

my shape is polished by faithful current
if I breathe deeply
open my pores
my spirit too is polished in this endless bath

trees shade me from sky above
scattering dark across water
like leaves sent to scurry over
no point other than the intimacy of touching

memories reach me from their source upstream
my sediment lifted from me
carried downstream
to become the future

will it know it is partly composed
from this moment's washing?

eventually I will be eroded free from this form
my grains ever smaller
my essence loosed of boundary
until I can say

now I am the river.

An orphaned child plucks rose petals
counts hidden blessings:

they love me
they love me not
first I was left
then I was bought

they love me
they love me not
sometimes I pay
for sins
of my old family lot

they love me
they love me not
I am the stew
gaining season
in the great boiling pot

they love me
they love me not
my road has lacked
rest but my breast
is made whole

shaped by the fields
flowering askew
carved by the blades
of fate turned anew
pledged by change
to become something
more

covered in clay
by hands of the day
rinsed to a shine
by purpose revealed
over the yonder
forward till healed

bronzed in the cauldron
fired in the sun
a fast talkin'
high steppin'
soul on the run

I could not have known
the depths of true love
without first tasting
loss and learning again
to stand by the fence
in the strongest wind
and not let go

and not let go.

The runaway youth
turns over achingly
a mountain of burden
avalanching cracked cares
deep into the mattress
of night

then
dawn breaks
a golden yoke erupts
into the yielding black
cobalt floods the morning
an epiphany flies through
his mental window and gives him
fresh peace for the day

for a lifetime:

I cannot get that over there
so I have to get this over here

I cannot taste the sweetest fruit
under my evading sun
so I have to taste all the sweetness
in the bitter one

I can't hear the most beautiful song
so I have to find beauty
in the song sung wrong

I can't shine what I don't have
so I have to shine what's mine

I have to sing my own song
paint my own portrait
plant my own garden
pick my own fruit
unearth my root
break my bread
find my water

and then

find out that what's my own
isn't mine alone

some soul somewhere
and I share

a song
a portrait
a garden
a fruit
root   bread   water

I am not alone
my own is not mine alone
I am a simple thread
in a crazy pattern
a wild wick
in a blazing lantern

I am not alone
I am the world
and all of this
is rays of bliss

when I shine what's mine.

Daydreaming beneath the willow tree
imagining himself as father horse
encouraging boy horse at his knee:

Young colt weary
from weight
of early life's hazard
sniffing scent of some
peaceful beyond
as long legs stretch and stride
from wobble to steady gait

nature's dawn brings thaw
to the crisp white grass
licking your hooves

softer passage awaits
you along your path

filling your strong lungs
once more with chilled
morning air

you pause and reflect
on your day of birth
then gallop on
with hints of full-grown
stallion in your manner
always searching
for your peaceful beyond

out there
beyond somewhere.

Far on the emerald meadow
strolling through ropes of breeze
the mentor asks the homeless youth

why do you love these horses so much?

the youth obliges with a smile:

a wild horse is a beautiful thing
it will not ask human permission
to be or sing

such brazen steed doubts not its freedom
all the world its rightful range
boundless roaming does not come strange

a penned up horse is not the same
its muscles surge at swing of stable gate
but doubt befalls its forward gait

first steps tremble at the fate
of crossing beyond the binding fence
that is its comfort zone

a penned up horse
abdicates its majestic throne

I too have become like this
afraid to gallop into my truth
shrinking before the open gate

freedom is a dream sown
into the imagination
of those who own
their dreams and all they hold
who set loose their fantasies
and dare live bright and bold

a wild horse is a beautiful thing
it does not ask human permission
to be or sing

nor bare its nature
nor rear and run

I dream of life like this
free and racing with the sun.

I am of my root
my root is of me
we can never truly be divided
we shall feed each other forever

I am because you were
you are because I still am

I am beautiful
because I was born of beauty

I am flawed
and the child of flaw

I have a lesson
because of what I saw

I have a song
not kept by the law

I am a winged thing
and will have my way

I am sunlight
punctuating turbulent day

I am compassion
tendering on life's flaming grill

I can open and trust you
if you dare and will

I am the fruit
that fell from the tree

that split open my bounty
at the foot of a glory

only I may decipher

what you call my agony
I call my piper

I am led by what
has befallen my fate

soon I'll arrive
at my potential's gate

swing wide the doors
jump in the pool

we'll all have a party
till some sensible fools

tell us it's time to hush
all the noise

that's when I'll tell you
the secret to girls
the secret to boys

no   let me tell you now
too many young
need you to know this

feed them what they *are*
and they'll become
what they *be*
purposeful
powerful
possibility

life's newborn miracles
grow in a field
only young spirits
love to visit

let us allow them
their roots
when they go there
to pluck them

they may return
to us with hands full
of bouquet and
daydreams
to last a lifetime.

Me and my friends
used to play in mud puddles
whenever we could catch them

since the flood
I don't think I'll play
in mud puddles anymore
I don't have a sad song for you
I just don't like remembering the mud
the oozing water
the things stuck inside

I like remembering the laughter we
passed around like bread
the wild things we dared
the shadows we fled

seeing traces of myself in other faces
makes me feel like
God took up some good clay
made some masterpieces
and kept the crumbs to the side
to make up me

I like feeling like I'm the leftovers
of some delicious meal
so much better than feeling like
I'm the first and only of my kind
something nobody's seen or tasted before

sometimes people swallow such food
just to be polite
I want people to see me and salivate
because they've had something like me before
and they *loved it*

I want to be the familiar stew
the favorite cake
the comfort food

I want to be the family recipe
passed down for generations
not on yellowed paper
but from heart to heart

when the flood came
I suddenly
washed up on somebody's plate
a strange and foreign food
nobody recognized that I came from
a batch that remains inside of me

I don't need to be stuffed with new recipes
to come out all right
I need someone to taste *my* original recipe
and find that even through the flood
I am *still* a delicacy.

Your Honor
I am nine years old
and not sure what a forever family is
or a loving home

I thought I had those things before

now you ask me whether
standing here today
I can truly say
I want to stay with this new family
I have come to know

if it means I don't have to stand up here
alone again in a court like this
I say yes

if it means I am no longer somebody's case
I say yes

if it means no more home visits
that my friends ask me about
I say yes

if it means I get to keep all my stuff
I say yes

if it means I get to keep my language
I say yes

if it means I get to keep my school
my teacher my grade my friends
I say yes

if it means I get to stop being labeled
I say yes

if it means somebody will help me
remember my dear family
I say yes

if it means I can make mistakes
and not be returned like merchandise
I say yes

if I can keep my pet turtle
I say yes

if someone will tell me my high
cheekbones are beautiful
I say yes

if I get to go to family reunions
and not be whispered about
I say yes

if someone takes the time to understand
what life is like for me
I say yes

if I get to wake up and remember where I am
I say yes

if I don't have to stop missing my first family
I say yes

Forever and Love are words
big people put on posters
to talk about children like me

me
I don't trust words on posters too much
I trust the little things that make me feel big

I trust big things that don't make me feel little

I trust the truth even if it hurts
'cause it can't hurt me more than a lie

I don't trust tomorrow
I trust today

so
Your Honor
if staying with my new family means
my heart learns peace starting today

I Say Yes.

I am Spirit
come to tell you my story

although I passed into here
through Mother dear and Daddy faded
my days soon thereafter were cast in
shadows ill paraded

monsters leapt from beneath my bed
stole away my sleep
weary became my constancy

I without a blanket
to secure me from my tremble
began the growing of my pain
the first days did assemble

then four new hands took me in
woman tall and specked
with graying hair
man with cavern voice
who sings Amazing Grace
softly in my ear

new-Mama always says to me:
Baby Son   you are my throne
says she is regal
because she is graced with me

in these words I find comfort
like the fetal one I remember

when I flash back
and shadows invite themselves
into my room where I seek peaceful sleep
new-Daddy comes to me
soaks me in his arms
strums his vocal chords vibration deep

Amazing Grace . . .
carries me to tranquility

I once was lost
but now am found
was fearful but now I sleep

universe is made not from stillness
but from movement
is composed not of staleness
but of change
I descend from that ocean
was made to move from first wave
into this . . . circle of my begotten blessing

a part of me will always float in space
the rest of me will always drown
in this Amazing Grace

I think I know what *kinship* means
on this earth none are unrelated
related is the *definition* of Life

relationship is the act of spirit
recognizing itself in another
naturally loving the self inside the other

a joyful soul spends life
finding itself in others
what stupendous treasure hunt

relationship is fulfillment of destiny
me   new-Mama   new-Daddy
we are not family unusual
we are family *meant* to be

humanity's highest work is *to take care of*
to take care of is to recognize essence
honor and respect essence
recognize other-essence in our own essence
taking care of others *is* taking care of self

the beautiful ones who take care of me now
I shall return unto them their glory tenfold
by virtue of how I become the universe
and walk a peaceful soul

both young and elder are stationed
near the doorway between worlds
when we tend to either we are
performing maintenance on the hinges
that ultimately swing for us
we lubricate the passageway
of our own birth and passing

we sing that *my home is over Jordan*
yet young and elder occupy the shore
between mid-life and the river
the river of *taking care of*
not condescendingly

resentfully
false pride-fully
but humbly
gracefully
thankfully
enduringly

our reward may not now be so evident
but surely and truly if we lean forward
we will hear whisper of our Amazing Grace

both the cared for and the caretaker
once were lost and now
in caring are found

this is how our blindness
may come to see

I grow weary
need to find my rest

please
won't you carry me?

A child begs for our surrender into love:

Our teacher is the day

and in that day
sage trees massage the sky
for they discern that air
is their truest plumage
and not the leaf

our teacher is the day
for life abundant courts us
with its lessons

you fear unbridling
your heart before me
lest I pierce it for
the offering
yet your truest
wound comes
from that very
surrender to fear

show me your heart
and all it holds
for thereby may I know
you as human
and in that knowing
settle my unsettledness
about your purpose
on my path

for you in your humanness
are by default
the dust of my path
the length of my striding
the arc of my sojourn

the blood with which my feet
stain the road I traverse
is swelled with your corpuscle

my embrace of you
shall be evidence of . . . hope
for my greatest test
on this shallow plain
of earth
is that I see you
not as the air encircling me
but as my plumage
and in strutting you
I set me free

our teacher
is the day

the lessons blossom
endlessly.

Sleep took over me in a tangle of vines
and a shower of rainy drops

leaping down from umbrella of leaves
onto my dirt-streaked face

morning roused me with the same patter
of drops on my forehead mouth neck

in the gaining light I brushed my fingers
over my facial skin
my fingers returned darkened red

I realized the raindrop patter of prior night
was now the bloody patter of the dead

my bullet-torn schoolmate lodged himself
in the trees above me during night

he knew he was dying as he nested there
like an old elephant he found his final resting place

he left me a final letter
his blood a mournful goodbye across my face

in the mud of a far-off place
I buried him in the weeping grove

my nineteenth goodbye since my family burned
in our straw home at dinner time

I was fifteen   my face lined
with a man's wrinkles worry wrought

greed and seduction dug the trenches of our war
bullets and bayonets dug the trenches where
my schoolmates now rest forever
grief dug the trenches in my heart

foreign governments dug my country's grave
with their *non-engagement*

memories dug the canals through which
my brothers and sister crawled back to me
mostly at night   mostly when the palms
grew heavy with rain   sagged and sighed

forest animal shrieks and howls
sometimes became merged
with dreamt cries of my family burning
while the nuts I had picked that day
lodged in my throat
pillowed in my mouth

by age eight my hands calloused
at the machete handle from clearing fields

at sixteen my calluses were killing pads
for an AK-47   my inseparable comrade
in the war that swept me up   held me tight

now I overdose on books about conquerors
on elephants in the Pyrenees
to keep the stench of horror from my mind

now I am calloused of heart as people
from dainty lives give me their smiles
and meals and pride   seeking to stroke me
into healing   growing ever impatient
with my emotional hide

now I lay me down to sleep
bound with five blankets
lest my soul to creep
back to the groves where rain changed
in the night to blood

and banished me from the season
where children find their normalcy

now I stow grain seeds beneath my nails
anticipating days without food
despite the dainty ones
piling mountainous meals
on the dining table and smiling
at me

back when I was seven
before mother left for heaven
she let me plant a garden beside her own

cabbage   squash   melons ripe
carrots   yams   corn delight

each morning I dirtied my knees
to tend and weed   turn and water
I saw how roots mingle in the earth
and child stalks survive beetles sun wind
even birth

I am sure the hate that singed our land
turned our gardens black and left them sand

I wonder though if by some miracle
the roots remain
shocked and shaking in the soil

if such a thing is possible
hope may live
for the calming of my pain
and I may learn again
to love the patter of falling rain.

Dear Madam University President, I am writing you this letter to indicate my desire to be admitted to your school for the fall 2008 academic year. I submitted my application to the admissions office as required, but at age 17, and after 12 years in foster care and 7 foster care placements, I have learned that it is best to state my intentions to any and everyone who might have a stake in determining my future. I would like now to present to you my qualifications for admission as a student to your university:

I was taken from my mother at birth
a rose plucked from earth
I have spent 17 years developing
a capacity to overcome loss
I laid baby brother in his grave
said goodbye to 9 best friends
I believe these meet your requirement
for what is called resiliency

I work well in relationships
10 social workers have walked with me
11 foster parents have fretted over me
5 ministers 4 pastors 3 priests 2 deacons
a medicine woman and a fortune teller
have prayed over me

if you need a student leader I'm the one
desperation to survive gave me a voice
and the will to use it
I am resourceful and will seek out
campus resources I require
just as I have had to do to make
my way through the child welfare system

and how would I get along with my
dormitory roommates?
I have already had 27 roommates
if you count my foster siblings

I possess strong writing skills
I have written long poems of prayer and desire
across my own heart in the black nights
that chased away my sleep

I deal well with turning negative into positive
caring adults too numerous to count
have condescended to me
from this I learned the grace such that
should my professors condescend to me
with low expectations
I shall return to them only my dignity

I know you are looking for team players
good campus citizens
I understand how important it is
for people to feel secure in their relationships
this has been the desert I have crossed
from family to family   friend to friend
I will make every student I come across
feel valued valid and full of voice

I have no choice
these are the things I need
to deny them to others would be hypocrisy
this is what foster care has made me see

blood ran red from rivers of self-mutilation
I carved into my flesh the story of my strife
but from this I learned the recipe for healing
now my rivers run as passion for music and history
both take me beyond my pain
on a journey of jazz soul and human reciprocity

I am not afraid to ask questions in the classroom
questions were my only protection
from the flawed intentions of my care providers
of my authorities

I am good at problem solving
trouble shooting and strategizing
I created *my own* case plan
so planning my course of study is no great task

enduring all night study sessions
are child's play to me
I have spent a thousand nights
studying my escape from life's limbo

I am a kite in flight
social pressure   what you call conformity
is but a flimsy string to me
I snap as I soar to my destiny

forgiveness? easy
my daily meditation is forgiveness
for those who abandoned me
made fun of me   judged me
scorned me   labeled me
gave up on me   ran scared from me

trust? who better than a foster child
to have the courage to trust
when so many times people have
done nothing but cause hurt and pain?
I withstood that bitter rain
learned to keep the water
let the salt run down the drain

compassion is a shelter I found
from the storms of my troubles
helping others on campus would be a reflex to me
a mentor lives inside me
this I already see

charity is often thought to be
the *giving* of a gift
but too often I have been the *object* of that charity
I know the truth
to be charitable is to honor the beauty of another soul
thereby opening yourself up to that beauty
receiving its hidden gift
when we help another
we are not *giving* charity
we are *receiving* it
from life's great beauty waiting within

I'm an A-plus student of sincerity
people have always felt the need
to be dishonest with me
they say oh we only want the best for you
and   your roots aren't worth talking about
and   if only you would bond or attach to us
your problems will be solved
your trouble flushed
I knew better
I crushed
dishonesty on the path to intimacy
with my own reality

I was a child of pain as much as of joy
both were my story
that I will tell the world

I will educate myself
craft my own Declaration of Independence
a Song of Interdependence
of the importance of relationship
my declaration will be a cry for truth
a drumbeat for honesty
a distaste for prejudice

as a teacher of what it means to overcome
I will claim my nobility
I'm cold corrected
make crazy beats from the basement of my destiny
and the rest of me
yeah it's dusted and rusted but it sure isn't busted
I just need a chance to find romance
in the way I learn to love this world
that's tripped me up

triumph over trouble is my cup
and my cup runneth over the rubble
I can make rose gardens rise from toxic grounds
I *must* have skills
I am not a tarnished adjective
I am a positive noun
I can't slow down   I'm almost there   where?
to Peace and Possibility
to becoming the whole of me

I've attended 14 schools
learned 198 foster family rules
had to catch up on spools and spools
of foster family stories and allegories
rituals and routines

had to tolerate a whole rack of
family tastes in food   music   threads
not to mention make all those beds
had to swallow my own song 158,716 times
been reprimanded for committing the crimes
of not learning my foster families' songs fast enough
not opening up and trusting quick enough
not forgetting the past enough
not conquering my pain enough
not smiling enough

not being grateful enough
not talking enough
not forgiving enough
for all sorta stuff
but mainly for being too rough . . . around the edges
so everything I touched tended to bleed
that's my main crime   I do concede

I had to polish up myself
learn to get along   go along
wait a long . . . time
before my own needs are quenched
this is evidence of capacity to endure   to cope
to not require immediate gratification
all reasons I can succeed at your university

I believe once I start college I'll major in
biology chemistry psychology sociology
history physics economics communications
english foreign language creative arts
and most of all politics
because I've already developed the skills
those majors require
just to get through my childhood

my *life* is my résumé
sure as sunlight seeks the day

Madam University President   if I may share with you
a summary of what I have learned from my time
in the system about the nature of human relations
that lesson is this:

the child in need is not the mouth we feed
the wound that bleeds   the soul that grieves
the falling leaves

no   a child in need is the fertile seed
the sacred creed   the unpolished bead
the opposite of greed   the lie now freed
to sprout from seed

when we teach mentor   raise guide this child
it is *WE* who are blessed *OUR* soul caressed
our stress less messed   *our* restlessness made less
our own pain finessed   *our* cold places warmed
in the breast of chest   *our* tenderness less suppressed
our callousness regressed *our* prejudice confessed
and given rest   *our* fears past crest
our special-ness dressed and pressed
our Truth made spark   then flame then zest
from that passion   springs the rest
our fullest shining   humanness

So, Madam University President, I am writing you this letter to introduce you to a child of the system, and I humbly submit to you that *precisely because of* my life journey, I am *exponentially* qualified. This is my story. I hope you have enjoyed the ride.

I journey
bold and bright
make my bed by
folding up the night

I sit on moon
ponder stars
play my dreams
like lofty music bars

kiss waking sun
who smiles and
walks with me

a flower shy and bright
blossoms on the path

it wears my blushing face

I am found
and home at last.

Beneath the bridge   in the rain
still far from the warmth of dawn
the mountainous voice rose from earth:

Your soul pours out now
you've suffered so long
all you needed
was to stop your madness of motion
and sit beside the grass

see how I have made it a shocking green
for you?

see how I have tinted the light
as in a dream?

this waking life is the true dream
a fantasy if you let it be

let go the chaos of lost souls
don't join that parade
I made you for the ecstasy of dissolving
in long baths of solitude
that your soul may awaken to its belonging
with all things

you must walk through the blistering
waterfall of loneliness
absolute chilling aloneness
before you reach the other side
where I make days a dream

the souls who circle you chattering
these are your angels at work
deciding how to entice you to hear
true music and leave alone the noise
of human wailing

bear for a moment the pain of separation

once you tear your self from flesh
you will open up into your final fantasy
realizing only then that you have always
been in the company of Creation
you could not be less alone

you are the center of the largest party
here there is no other
for all exists within you
all around you is come from your own breath

taste the mint leaf
you were the one who gave it sweetness
the smell of jasmine is from your own scent

stop wasting your whole life seeking others
racing behind the parade like a panicked child
afraid no one will notice you

you are the parade
it is your panic that goes unnoticed
parades stop not for the forlorn

you are not left in the desert
you are the desert's leavings

sip my hidden water and rise up
from this taunting earth.

Barefoot in the sand of dunes
bathed in the blushing sky of dawn
dressed in white linens flapping gently
a young man and woman face each other
to be wed

the groom   on the verge of this
the first true family of his whole life
shakes before the one to be his wife
makes his vows:

I am a hollow reed
in the hands of Love

she shall play me
as she chooses

my grain polished
in her natural oil

her wind a rustling
wave through my instrument

I was shaped long ago
refined through strategic seasons

her lips were always ready
for this moment of my arrival

little could I have known
that in the summer heat
and the cicada choir
she would be my survival

moon sets fat
morning balloons to brightness

this day is come
into my breast and perched

I am the wild one
braying at the sky

I am the settler
on the dusty trail
who never questions why

I am the recalcitrant longing
now letting go

I am the crying rain
I am the melted snow

I bent down to pick up
a precious stone
and picked up God's Intent

my heart shuddered
now I feel Me dent

my tin pan stands no chance
my chalice is set to weep
my steel drum is welted
my furnace no longer sleeps

Love is blowing her
mint breath through
my waiting reed

music leaves from
my every opening
I astounded at the deep

I never knew
such a hollow place as I
could be filled like this
so blown open
so flooded Godly
and of Grace.

The eight-year-old stands
before her class
draped in a flowered dress
beaming with revelation almost
unseen in such youth

she has no notes   no props

she begins:

my grandmother is in the trees
so I go to the trees
smell their bark
scent of her perfume escapes the wood

child pauses a moment to gauge their reaction
silence
so she continues

my favorite doggy is in the grass
I go and sit on the soft blades
there I can pet him and stroke him

my Aunt Chalice   she is in the water
I go down by the creek
and play with her
she always tickles my feet

my babysitter is in the fruit trees
in our backyard
I pick a peach or pear everyday
slowly eat it
babysitter always kisses me
makes me feel good inside

my baby brother   he is in the garden
I go and sleep there
when the sun is out

he tells me   secrets
from inside   the blossoms
of the flowers   from the bosom
of tomatoes   from the foot of cornstalks

he lets me know when rain is
coming or when the soil is lonely

more silence   then the teacher asks
how are these people where you say they are?

and the eight-year-old   finishing her turn
at show-and-tell   answers with surprise:

where else do you think they would go
when they leave us?
they pass into the places we love
so they can be with us forever

returning to her seat
she thinks to herself contentedly
and with a smile
where have these people been all their lives?

At the end of the school year
the young man sits and shares
with his favorite teacher what he has learned
about having someone believe in you:

I allow my mind
to describe a rock
and am left more able
to imagine the grain it bears
too   the mountain whose earth it shares

the object is not life's nectar
the gathering of it is

the place is not the point
how we occupy that place is

the way is not so glorious
our walking of it is

you sang me your song
and thought I was your audience
I was the notes your lips ushered

your breath was my coat
its moisture my skin I shed
as I left you and became cloud
it was like stepping from a warm
bath and evaporating

what I became was not so important
as the fact that I did

change.

Story time   and the 15-year-old mentor
shares with her pensive young friend
a tale of how she sees both their lives:

So the story goes
small tender-hearted baby
born to his mother dear
in the desert
by the river

taken from the womb
to the post-natal room
then foster care
then adopted into a home
with the expectation that
he not let his Truth shine out

that he not speak about it
think about it
feel about it
be about it

and though he was well loved
the pain
it came   never ending flood
in sheets of rain
no relief
just private tears
and pillow stains

and he asked
the small child
he asked

God
why hast thou forsaken me?
why am I alone?

and God answered
child of Mine
I have not forsaken you
I have given you life

I have torn your world
asunder
this is My Divine plan
not a simple blunder

you must be cast in this fire
for I need you to be
a certain stone

only this fire
can bring the right shine
to the light of you I need

you must have patience
though the nights are long
you must endure
like My child Job
you must endure

you must have faith
though the light
has yet to dawn before you
you must believe with
the depth of My child Abraham
you must believe

you will see
My child
you are not alone
for I am with you
in the streets
and in the home

the pain you feel
is My path laid down for you
walk it to Me
you are the salt
I am The Sea

and the day came
when the child
became a man
and found his voice
and in speaking
a woman who heard his voice
came to him

she was Black as fertile earth
and weary from wear
her eyes watery
her body shaken by the touch of light

and it was God
who spoke through her
and said
child
you are *Moses*
taken from your people
at birth

so that you may live
among those who strain to see
the whole of you
and see the truth in their heart
know the true breadth of humanness

this has given you sight
unlike others into the truth of
your own heart and that of your people

you have come to know the Divine
meaning of your people's pain
for their pain has been returned to you
a hundredfold

you have swallowed this ocean of tears
kept it close by your heart
that you may not stray
from My plan for you

you must go forth
and speak of what you have known
you must tell your people
that God has spoken these words

and God spoke such:

behold   a certain number of souls
children born into the abyss
where children are not meant to be

you must not feel sorry for these children
feel responsible for these children
for within them lies a truth restless
for daylight

I have borne them a pain
that has given them a vision
and among them
are ones who will
rise up among their people
and serve as teachers
messengers
leaders

take notice
of these children
for beyond the stories
of abuse   neglect   poverty
violence   disease
they are Moses in your midst

where despair is in the life of a child
you must bring that child home
for there is Moses in your midst

take care with these tender souls
for these children shall go forth
as a people with passion in their hearts
and a great vision
for I have
spoken early into their ears
you shall be unto Me a holy nation

where a child is left un-kept
you shall keep her
where a soul is left in tatters
you shall bring repair

mourn not your loss
of comforts as you comfort
lives in need
for your needs shall be satisfied
by My Divine breath
which shall fill you up
and make you whole
exceedingly

you shall be that cloud
above
unencumbered
for you will have fulfilled My word

and where they bid you
do your works for private gain
respond with a soulful heart
and actions for public good
make your neighborhoods a temple
unto your kin

feed into your homes
lessons of your people's legacy
stories of miracle and wonder
let no child be unexposed
to the possibility of triumph
over pain

let no child dance alone
as I have made their joy
a thing to be witnessed
their celebrations a cause
for you to pause your frantic pace

let no dream from children
fade in the morning
to be not captured in the net of day
for child dreams
are My bounty from the sea
harvest them well
do not assume that I will
always make the sea so plentiful

even when these children
pull from you in fear
extend yourselves to them
make of your arms
a bridge they may cross
they seek a way
over troubled water
play well your part

let no child song be solo
in its singing
join them in that breath of joy
let them know their melody
is a good one
they have music to offer the world

if they believe they are needed
they will rise up like morning glories
and stroke the sky
with beauty you have never known

keep no dust upon their shoulders
from inattention
make them feel your eyes
constant upon their backs

that they are known
they are seen
they are cradled
in your love and care
and respect
for all the days

they will test your resolve
these children
as I have tested theirs
for faith is made of
painful things

but watch for their produce
for I shall give unto them
manna bread that only they may harvest
and bring into your homes
one day it is they who will
fill your plates and sustain you

shepherd them all the way
of their path
for they lead you into the place
where the sea is parted
on the left and on the right
and through which you must pass
if ever your kind will find freedom

if ever the screams of slaves
shall be pulled wet from the sea
and made into freedom's exclamation

if ever the warriors cut down
as they stood for your dignity

are to testify in that Higher court
on the day of your long last justice

if ever the rose thorns that
have insulted your skin
all these generations
are to bear blossom
and bathe you in the fragrance
of children faring well

if ever you are to
find faith in that I am
the wood
and I am the stone
that is your home

and
that *I am that I am*
that these children
are that I am
therefore as you
reclaim their sense
of safety and security
you recapture your own
chance of salvation

for a new season has come
these are days of endless nights
and your sleeping time
should cause you shudder

too many injured adult souls
seep discernment from their vessels

such seepage
floods good homes
into the waters of jeopardy
such that the tide
flows through bedrooms
and lifts children
from where they lay

and out the door
into the vastness of systems made
not from the substance
of your people's legacy
but from hearts and minds
in blind lurch and stumble

know that
when those who would oppress
your people build vessels
whose charge is to carry your
own children to salvation
the only consequence is
these vessels will come
to hold your children in life's limbo

and neither transport them to a better
shore nor return them back to
the first shore restored

when those who would oppress
your people build vessels
to carry your children
beware that *I* have not built
those vessels

they are crafted of the impulse
of imperfect men
and what you inherit from
that manner of lumber
is not My word
nor My way

but the word and way
of a spirit who would
lash that lumber so
leakage may steal aboard
and drown your precious offspring

I have given you
My word
and My way
since long ago
before this land you call free
you have always
cared for your children
according to My Heavenly inspiration

It was I who whispered
creativity into your ears
upon which you found ways
even in your struggles
to make good hearted people
a part of your family
even without the bond of blood
kinship is your word for this

I call it My Divine order
for you shall love your neighbor
as yourself

and family is a richness
you can not inflate

It was I who tapped
truth into your hearts
that you would speak stories
to your young ones of values
and lessons they must gain
to grow to productive lives
in a world where foe and friend
speak with same tongue
a world where their origins might
be cause for their destruction
a place where their ways
might be seen as less than human
their spirituality spat away in fear

who knows better
the substance your children
will require than you who have
survived upon that same stalk
in your endless storm?

where you go
in seek of answers to broken
hearted children
go first unto yourselves
for there is where the hearts
were broken first

go not to those
who would dictate to you
a recipe for their own taste

where you would build a home
make it for a child
where you would grow a family
make it for a child
where you create community
make it for a child
where you construct a temple
make it for a child

for where I am worshipped
must you make a home
for My children

do yourselves this favor
because with these children
there is Moses in your midst

for every child who cries
let there be a family
who would teach the ways of love
and self love
how to conquer prejudice
and give one's life for one's people

let your lessons flow
from your every mouth
and drip from your cloth
to puddle around your every step

for the moment you
leave that footprint behind
a child takes to hands and knees
and drinks from that water hole

be   ware
there drinks Moses in your midst

let there be for every shelter
one child dream to protect
one dawn for every darkness
one feast for every hunger
one family for every solitude
one community for every family
one people striving for one truth
one love for one purpose
one faith in the value of every life
one hope for one fear
one joy for one tear
one peace for one war
one home for one life run wild
one temple for one blessed child

each one
Moses in your midst
give them shelter
they will give you
manna from My Heaven
freedom from My fist

careful with them

careful

they are
Moses in your midst.

Youth illuminates guardian
during their weekly walk through woods:

When autumn leaves fall from trees
they beautify ground
fertilize earth
become substance for new birth

when we children fall from families
we too can beautify the ground
we just need someone to
hold us sacred for who we are

your tears of sympathy
rot our leafiness

your celebration
breaks us beautifully
down to earth

in that sacred soil
we fallen child leaves
cup ourselves
to carry extraordinary

we mimic the triumph
of sprouts who breach
soil's crust
we become fertile
and all the while
gorge on youthful wanderlust.

Stage left
a quiet brook

stage right
a nightingale on the look

down stage
the sweetly melancholic youth
begins his soliloquy
in the final gloaming
beneath a satiated orb of moon:

culture
does anybody know your essence?
you claw like creeping vines
through blood and bones
saturate the walls
where humans dwell
cast elusive spell
like petroglyphic
love sonnets
written in child's
white chalk script
in black of
deepest cave

culture
you make us crave
love
I love it when you talk like that
love
I love it when you stroke my back

love
I love it when you take my child heart
in your hands and caress
the topography of my . . . love

you don't try to shape
my heart in your hands
like so much passive clay
squeezing gray dying through
the breaches between your fingers
you know that would
rupture creeping vines within
this pumping glistening
condensation of a stream
that holds direct VIP status
with Creation

and therefore goes my . . . culture
does anybody know your breath
as it takes its scent within my mouth?
and who around here knows
your tendency to curl in warm currents
through my mind

making thoughts dance
like jitterbugging jukebox playing
gin swigging
common folk
in the sweat box
of a crammed joint by the
mosquito clouded river
on a full moon August night?

oh my flutter taking flight

making my thoughts
dance like fresh oil
on the water coated griddle
like rain drops popping
off taut tense trampoline
of a hairdo done
with too much pomade?

like sweetness
doing calisthenics
in my lemonade?

dance like
I child see world with eyes
naïve and wild
make whole picture fresh
like mama's bestest apple pies
make old ways
bring silly questions to my mind

like if you say you love me
why do you run from
my creeping vines?

is love therefore
the condensation
of the chemistry
between affection
and discomfort
browned in the oven
of intellectual confusion
blackened over the
broil of emotional fear?

and should this be that
meal that carries me
lifts me
makes my soul
swell from deflated balloon
to brazen plump and mighty
planet that in adult form
seeks to orbit according to
the essence of my culture?

do I drift?
let me say it like this
when I touch my lips
that minute act has roots

when I cry at purple sky
emotion comes from a place
that lives
maybe not in your time
or your place
or your people   heart   home   dreams

my emotion
comes from a place that lives
and seeds with a million
billowing strokes
of fertility
the soil   rain   sunlight
that give the Divine right
for my creeping vines
to vein my heart
stain my eyes
wane the storm
of my discontent

for my culture
smells like this   tastes like this
feels like this   grows like this

and comes from
comes from
molecule   ionic particle
atomic dance   spirit romance
across the ages
turning pages
of generation
to leave I child
in your hands
not as clay
but as a truth
that comes from
a place that lives

pray I every moment
of every night
that as I child
am in your hands
you put away your
crushing grasp

and love my
I mean bleed and love my
I mean humble and love my
I mean thank Divine Sky
and love my
creeping
vines . . . .

What were you imagining
when you brought me to the place
that for you is home?

you could not have been thinking
of me
I am the last thing
this place is

I am a copper storm of tears
beating against your cold window

the slew of my pieces
falls down wailing against
the glass

I am beating
both to get in and to catch
your attention

the woods of this non-seeing
are swallowing me

your closed conception of me
opens a door for the wolves to enter

your fear is a pallid finger
stirring a vortex into existence
your avoidance a sharp breath
gusting me to cusp of flush

you know the next step don't you?

many things drown in the ocean
often unnoticed or misdiagnosed

most of us are too busy to notice
the nature of a drowning
we aren't looking directly at
the soon to be departed

her thrashing escapes our periphery
this is how we would have it
for to truly notice a drowning and do nothing
is a tortuous death itself for the nothing-doer

I am the night's bleating rain
against your cold window

I make patterns like ant columns
in the sand on your hard glass
as I fall

I do not fall intentionally
this is not manipulation
that would require my belief
that you would catch me

I am headed down the glass
to the graveyard of souls deposed

and what were you imagining?
my compassion ends this poem:

perhaps we both can recover
if we leave our souls on the fire
to become something new.

Can I call you Mom?
not just when the sun is shining melancholy
and the house is full of laughter honey sweet
but also when my fear becomes a monster
from which I cannot retreat
can I call you Mom?

when the wind whistles to me that I
am something cast away and I respond
with sullenness or simply surrender to
the breaking waves upon sifting shores within
my breast   can I call you Mom?

I know you're there for me when I get good grades
and take out the weekly trash
but when I find messy ways to lick my wounds
from being discarded like that trash
can I call you Mom?

will you wait for my bluer sky?
for my waterfall to come?
I fear you will give up on me like others did
like others do
that's why I'm steady testing you

I need to see the boundary of your faith in me
my soul searches endlessly
for the proof that I am truly loved
not just parts of me but the whole of me
all of me needs to find a meadow where
I can finally rest peacefully
can I call you Dad?

will you do more than play catch with me?
will you cradle me in your gentle sea?
rock me gracefully into my sleep at night?
or will your heart give up on me
when we fight or see this world in different light?

does my pain have a passport to live here too?
or will you deny my hurt at the door
making me drop my tears silently? privately?

if so I fear I will drown having never swum
in your gentle sea
so if I'm rude or wrong or just plain bad
can I call you Dad?

when other children scorn the skin of me
will you actually be there for me?
will you bleed with me?

I know people look at me and see
a tornado spinning recklessly
will you look and see the truth of me?
will you? will you see the all of me?
or am I only in your eyes to be
the imitation of your own beauty?

I've been bouncing through this world
like a basketball but no one wants to
take a shot with me
no one believes I can find the hoop
that I can score
but if you just send me on my proper arc
I know I can win the game
can I call you Mom and Dad?

or does fostering the whole of me
make your soul run sad?
will you let me take my story out from
under the bed and share it in the living room?
or will our family sweep away my truth with
avoidance broom?

can I bring my passions with us to the park?
you like the rising sun
I like star gazing in the dark

can I pull my fears from the sock drawer
and show them to you?
or will you consume yourself with convincing me
that I have nothing to fear in your loving home?

my fears are real but if you won't allow
me them honestly
that would be my monstrosity
see I need to know if you are down with me
down in the trench where I walk through life

that way   with your company   I'll have the strength
to cut through my strife   leave the trench
I'll find my solid ground   learn to shine my light

can you   will you   foster me?
will you let me foster you?
I can show you new things too
like how to love an imperfect soul
in a way you never thought you'd do
and if ever it were meant for you and I to part
I pray that you would rest peacefully

knowing that for a priceless season
you gave this child   me   a reason to believe
he could make it in this world

because when I talked you truly listened
when I shined it was your heart that glistened

when I ached inside you never lied
about your heart's frustration
you let my trauma breathe
become my own salvation

because you let me sing my song
even if you didn't know that tune
you let me love October
just like you love June

because you found the courage to face your
prejudice about that part of me
that discomforted you
because you did not treat me as charity
but as your Golden Opportunity

because you realized that you did not just
foster me but that I also fostered you
because in your hands   your humble hands
I found that meadow where I discovered
that I am beautiful and that I belong

because you fought the bitter social wind
and swam upstream on my behalf

because of all of this you will have given me
my sweetest kiss   my forever bliss
my rainbow painted in words like this:

this child   this soul   withstood the rain
overcame the pain   caught the Glory Train
shall never return   to despair again

if this is what we are to be as family
I will walk this earth and make you proud
your imperfect beauty will always shine
forth from me

can I call you Mom?
can I call you Dad?
I can?
good
you can't see it
but inside my heart is glad

I Love you Mom
I Love you Dad.

Morning Mommy
Morning Daddy

I had a dream last night
it was a good dream
felt like cotton candy on my tongue
felt like my skin warm under morning sun

I was a big girl in the dream
I was a mommy too
I was sitting in my white nightgown
during indigo night
under crescent moon

I was writing you both a letter
it went like this:

Mommy Daddy I remember my first kiss
the one you both gave me that first
night in your home when you tucked me in

you both kissed me on my lips   at the same time
it was then I knew that you were mine
my first kiss it felt like this:

like I was a rose and   all my thorns just
dropped to the ground   it was a song
an amazing sound   it felt like grace
amazing grace   had come to me

it felt like my tears were now the sea
felt like floating on the ocean wide
felt like crossing over to the other side

the side where children don't have to
run and hide   the side where bacon scent
fills the house at sunrise   and I'm not scared
no more to wipe the sleep from my eyes

'cause I know this day will greet me good
with sweet tea and harmony between my
family and me

it felt like a promise of something glowing
like rust washed from around my heart
felt like my panic slowing

felt like rain that knew my dry spots
like wind   sweet breeze that carried me
like ground for once beneath my feet

like rainbows dancing
the sky a brilliant blanket sheet
my first kiss   it felt like this

the next morning my life with you began
I remember things you thought I didn't know
I remember how you feared I wouldn't grow
to love you like you loved me so

feared my heart would freeze from past pain
and I would grow silent like winter snow
I heard your whispers through bedroom door
how you worried one day I would be
yours no more

but by then my heart had grown a place inside
for you   a garden for which your flowers
alone would do
I was a child but even I knew
my roots had taken hold in you

even if one day I would
have to leave your space
my heart's garden would always
be our family reunion place

I grew this in my heart for you
because when I cried
you kept my tears and used them
for a swimming pool
where we swam as
family in the substance of *my* life

you dared to get wet in what I was
dared to swallow my salt along with yours
showed me my water *is* clean enough for you

you kept my tears and filled a place
in your home with them
this was to be my reflection pond
a place at home where I could go and
see the image of myself

sometimes I looked ugly like a porcupine
some days I looked pretty and called myself
Clementine but every day I lived with you
you preserved my reflection pond so I could
see myself and know I was more than rumor
I was true

not only that   you drank from my pond
so I could see myself in you
you said so many times *we love you*
but I've heard such words before
then the truth was shown
that I was to be the cast out stone

it was only when you said the words
then swallowed me
that I truly believed I was
orchid floating in your sea

Ma and Pa   I remember my first kiss
the satin of your skin
pillows of your lips
coffee on your breath
Pa's hands on Mommy's hips

I remember that first kiss
doorway to my future bliss
now I am a mommy too
and I want to tell you what I've learned:

foster is a funny word
child comes to us a hummingbird
fluttering nervous tiny thing
frantic beating of her wings
hungry starving daring thing
darting dancing wishing she could sing
like other birds and have her song listened to
enjoyed . . . understood

child comes to us a hummingbird
flighty prancing hoping thing
praying this family will let her sing
searching for that safe place to land
finally able to rest her wings
those fragile resilient soulful wings

a child comes to us a hummingbird
a jazzy soulful freestyle groove
seeking our family nectar
dreaming of its sweetness inside her
private heart

she has come to us with *her* song
seeking *our* sweetness
this is reciprocity
we her family learn her song
sing it back to her all life long

she fills her vessel with harvest of a blessed home
moves forward with her wealthy life
she flies   full of us and fresh of wing
but she *must* fly   she is hummingbird
she has songs to sing

our love has become her
our love has *become* her
she sings new word
she is blessed grounded hummingbird

With that, the six-year-old kissed her mommy and
daddy on the lips and ran off to wash up for breakfast.
She smelled bacon in the house.

Her dream was good.

Her heart journal entry:

I too
have been to the mountaintop
you would not believe
the future I have seen

I have found the human heart

it grows in the Cave of Longing
just beyond the Woods of Belonging

you have to follow the River of Solitude
to find it beating in a Pool of Love

the cave is hidden
in a giant Moss of Fear

I know Solitude
therefore I can find my way
through Belonging

I can recognize Longing
when we get there

when we do we'll have to
trample down the Moss of Fear

I've done this before
I'll be your guide
to the human heart

Follow me.

More of her heart journal entries:

Everybody looks at me
nobody sees me.

Who writes the law
that says anyone who wants me
can have me?

I want a law
that says anyone who has me
has to want me

ALL OF ME.

They don't know this yet
one day I'll shine
they'll stop and feel
I am the eternal sunrise
I am
I be
I will.

People want to solve my problems
people are my problems
they need to solve themselves.

I am a pebble
bouncing between boulders
who believe they are stroking
me with feathers
their touch feels like stone.

I exist
behind the blinding mist
your prejudice
casts upon my bliss
look deeper and discover
I exist.

ice cream   dreams   promises:
things that melt away
I want to live in the place
where melted things stay.

I hear whispers
from far and aching shores
it is my great and distant Amma
she whispers to light a fire
and to keep me warm

even on sunny days
my heart is soaked with whispers.

On the upper left corner of the bunk bed
the corner up against the wall
she carved a series of musical notes
into the bed post with a spoon she took
from the kitchen and hid during the day
in the pouch of her stuffed animal kangaroo

each night she carved a single note
long after her new family had passed into sleep
the notes were flats and sharps and ran crooked
down the post from left to right

each note represented the substance of
that particular day as it melted into her
a mist snaking into the pores of her skin
becoming her

over a period of three years she kept
inscribing her daily passages like weather
reports on the soft fading wood
the post became a tattooed trunk
littered with a symphony

her new father noticed her etchings
so did her new mother
new brother cousin sister best friend
none knew their meaning

though each tried to ask
her answers were always the same:

these notes are my music
the music is my name
the music is my name

she told herself this
almost as a chant she bathed herself in
especially when pain battered against her heart
a monsoon of side-swept tears tearing
at the lake of emotion deep within

the music is my name

only she knew the meaning of this music
knew the beautiful truth of her name
it would remain a secret she kept tucked
like a love letter inside the folds
of her child heart

one day at the breakfast table
she announced to her new family:

these many days I have spent in this family
have been some of the richest of my life
you have been so good to me
yet I know I remain in your heart
and in the eyes of this community
cause for worry   rumor   stigma
carrier of a story that sheaths my truth

so now I want to introduce
you to my true name
that which I call myself
in music on my bedpost
and in the auditorium
of my private thoughts

silence around the table

I call myself this name to counter
the well intended silhouette that follows me
the ideas in people's minds that bend
their perception of my light into illusion

because you have been so kind to me
let me introduce you to my music
which is my truest name

she debuts her deepest soul and sings:

my blossom yawns
its morning dawns
unfolding of my flower
has seized the hour
what glory comes
a'splashing through
the light of this
newborn day

her family   stunned

she concludes:
the music is my name and . . .

my name is *Beautiful.*

We who walk the road of whispers
do render this
declaration of the adoptive child:

When grown bodies fail to nurture those draped in tenderness whose growing is incomplete and what's more has been disrupted by way of rupture, separation, dislocation, and transplantation, we so assaulted must act.

We hold in this place of conjure that men and women who have shed the unique skin of that most peculiar childhood should take hold the reins of self-definition in word, idea, and action, and set the course for freedom that their kin in circumstance would follow:

Freedom from abeyance by the fears of men; freedom from vulnerabilities of the latent voice of youthful in-articulation; freedom from quiescence before the agendas of those who have not walked that certain path; freedom from the withering erosion to esteem and identity come from stigma, prejudice, and devaluation on the basis of our life's occasion.

Freedom yet to tell a story and stand by the truth of it, no matter the offense to the sensitivities of the powerful or the moneyed; freedom from the blight of unjust tradition, dehumanizing conformity, and misguided missives.

Above all that we should set the course for freedom to live among the world of children as divinely worthy of but the best that adult-kind can hew from the mountainous disarray that is a child's life gone astray. For we are not special in the way that a comet is special amongst stars but special still in that the light of individual distinction and purpose shines within us, as with all children.

Our face is revealed on the slate hillside emergent beneath the receding glacier of myth. Our countenance is set in defiance against cast down eyes, for let it be known here and to the cusp of imagination's sweet limit that we are not charity, no pitiable soul-less mass. Who would adopt us has in fact presently been adopted *by us*. Our partnership is no less than equal. No more tarnished by the condescension of favor than is birth itself.

Look to the clamor on the horizon that is this global society's future. Our merriment if it strikes a wicked note upon the ear's drum is simply the sound of freedom at long last come. We know that look in the eyes of the adoptive one who has laid to rest her long nights of query toward life's providence. We know the daunting length of the circle traversed from birth to rupture to replant to reunion. We are intimate with the meaning of union, that lifelong consequence of choice: choice to shed away, rise, embrace, *become*.

We cast new light on biological strands in the quilt human and give hope to intimacies of the spirit. We are evidence of the fragility of bonds and contentment, even as we are whisper of resilience. Desolate is not the substance of our heart. The precise health of peace is our comportment to no lesser degree than for any other child or child of childhood, for childhood's season too spawns its own offspring in the form of adult complexities.

This is a tale of gleaming opportunity and fertile ambivalence. The broken chains of our familial fabric rust themselves from neglect yet become our amulet of personality, like coral colonies grown bright and bountiful on the backs of broken leftovers in the sea. Our hearts take hold and surge forth brazen in the tide of our reconstituted sense of family.

Friction has shaped and fitted us with an eyepiece whose lens takes us deep into the heart of a child's pristine flower of insecurity. From this vantage it strikes us that we are the ultimate authority beneath only Divine Wisdom in that moment when souls strive to erect a home in theory, legislation, policy, action, and in a child's heart: A home tangible and intangible that would set the orbit of the adoptive child to its gloaming.

As that authority, we assert here that we as children shall not be the last of thoughts when adult-kind holds forth on our welfare. We shall be the beginning of thoughts and the ending centerpiece of thoughts. We hold that the fate of our possibilities shall not find its end beneath the residue of politics, policy, and finance. We will not be the inheritors as children of what older mouths spoke forth as barriers to our emancipation from drift.

Our storm shall be told in poetry and prose. Our thorns shall foretell the coming of our rose. Our every unique cultural truth shall be held in the light of society's scramble toward mature humanism.

We assert the right to have and express struggle with our circumstance without lambaste for daring ingratitude for the blessings of family that befall us. Cannot the ocean bemoan the weight of its belly even as it enjoys the splendor of its majestic bounty? We declare these things as solemn and true.

Our charge too is guided inward. Who goes forth from this uprooted garden should pain to find root in the forgiving earth of relationship. And family will be given a new name. This is our charge and bittersweet legacy. Bound are we by the fickle tether of our fate and who but Turmoil should render forth that river toward peace? The lamp is lit, for always is there a home for the one who would dare believe in love again.

We are not *the adopted*. It is we of anxious hearts and nimble dreams who do the adopting. And behold us not in language as *adopted*, for that is measure of a past and finished thing. We are more than that legal transaction, that moment of movement across an unsteady stream. No, we ought to be in language called *adoptive*, for our act of bonding with the familial branches of our totality is a vibrant, pulsing thing whose fingers grasp persistently at the fringes of tomorrow. So say we that we are active in this *adoptive-ness*, even into the autumn of our living years.

We are apple seeds planted too shallow in first soil, thus given to the wind to scatter. What seed is designed to thrive in the garden of its unfamiliarity but that bore of higher purpose? Whose choice is it that we germinate and rise? Whose sun bakes us whole even as the hole that bore through us early is caulked and filled with the leaf of loving honor, a leaf that chewed and dissolved, is the healing compound of our ages? Whose sprout left its bed, sleepwalked, resoiled? Who knows the battlefield of nightmares in which our self-love toiled and threw its mighty blows?

We have tasted the storm at the window, felt the shudder of the pane. Still we remain, nothing so special, and therefore special at that. For we are but every child. And that is the headline of our success. We have been raised, risen, and returned . . . faithfully to the garden that is our essence, to the orchard of our truth that shaded us from the broil above. To the rock of our spirit's resolve whose wide girth gave us a leaning place. We have not defaulted the race. We are in the race's mid-water stretch. That place in the ocean before sight of the shore, too far out to have satiation inside, too close to the truth to turn a callous chin.

We are the delta of many rivers, the dusk of many days. We are descendant complexity, spark of perplexity. All manner of mundane, tears of near surrender darting 'tween the rain. We speak mute, our lives explain.

When there is found, like footprints trailing afar, failure by those whose charge is the adoptive child to recognize and resoundingly respond to our particular drumbeat, then unequivocal is our responsibility and right to assert ourselves into that stand of self representation as to our story, nature, need, and chosen mode of existence.

Resolved are we in this, at this season's leading edge, backed against the precipice of misrepresentation. Doubt not that our stand will of need be deeply rooted and that our movement shall be forward toward revelation rather than backward toward misappropriation of our collective potential. Yet we seek the sun. Never in this shall we come undone. The course has been run and now it is the season of the adoptive child to forge into being new stories, documents, and interwoven missions that would so define our spirits' thrust.

This is our declaration, here birthed, and forever to evolve to its living, breathing, and divine potency.

Do you see me?
If so you seed me
I take root in you

do you feel me?
if so you feed me

I fill my well
with water clean

do you hear me?
if so you heal me

understanding is
the medicine I need

will you be my student?
if so I will teach

and in teaching
I will learn from you

in marriage two
make a sacred pledge as one

in this relationship
we cannot be

one without a pledge
from two

that you will
seek my magnificence

and I will
seek yours too.

She
skips rope to the beat
of chocolate milk surging
down a parched
12-year-old throat
in high July

her
bare feet bouncing for relief
off the street
heart beat moving fleet
dreams dancing in her head
of when her family will
be whole again
because she feels

if
we can just get it
together we'll be okay
cause we are family
can't nobody take that away from us
can they?

that night
in the glow of street light
hidden under the sheets
she takes pencil to paper
feeds her journal these words:

my greatest fears:

she writes
and as she writes the words
are also written on the blackboard
inside her mind
etched on the inner walls
of her heart
where they will stay
stubborn graffiti
hidden in the shadows
but persistent all the same

and she writes

my greatest fears:

Mommy dying
Daddy crying
bad things under the bed
somebody taking my family away
away

I know a way
to keep bad things away
I'll pray
I'll do like Ms. Johnson
at the library
when people come at her mean
I'll look at them scary
I'll build a wall around my heart
that way no fires can start
inside my chest
that would escape from
there and burn the rest of me

I'm afraid cause people
don't seem to like my family
they don't say so with their mouths
they speak it with their looks
wish I had me some cookbooks
for all the crooks who
come to steal our joy
I'd make me up a meal
so hot and spicy
they would have to ask us for water
least for once they'd be asking *us* for something
seems like we're always asking
somebody else for something

then they always give us that look
like we are something less
and they are something more
but they don't know my godmother
she can sing like an angel
they don't know my
best friend Keisha
can't nobody add
numbers as fast as she can

they don't know my Uncle Roy
I've seen him make a gourmet meal
from nothin' but flour and water
seem like to me

my Daddy he may not be fancy
but he can dance with Mommy
real sweet and make her feel like
somethin' special when he dips her down

and Mommy she may not have
all the best dresses and shoes
she may not talk smart-like
but she knows more ways to
stretch a dollar than those folks
in suits and nice cars always
stressin' they budget and fussin'
'bout they stocks and *bombs*

and my family
we sure can tell some stories
keep you laughin' most the night
stories 'bout folk we know
and some we don't
don't wanta know either
and stories 'bout Moses
and Ms. Harriet Tubman
and Jesse Owens
stories that make you feel
good about yourself
yeah we can light a fire
with stories and keep
the house warm 'til
morning light

I just hope nobody ever takes
me away
cause how would I ever find
my way back
and why are people always talking
about sending me to a better life
folk seem awful comfortable
with the idea of me never seeing
my family again

I read my books
I remember they used to do that
to slave children
send them away to a better life
I bet in the Master's house
when trouble came
the children didn't get sent
to a better life
seem like folk think children like me
weren't ever supposed to be with
their own families in the first place

yes'm
I read my books
they took certain other children away too
they called it making them civilized
they used to cut off all their hair
us   they take us and cut off our memories

but what if I don't want no better life?
what if I just want *my* Mommy
and to play with *my* brother
and keep going to *my* school
and never ever split up with *my* friends?

so what Mommy's not doing well
I'll go stay with Big Ma
she loves me too
and if not Big Ma
more than two people in my family love me
ain't that true?

I get so tired I just want to sleep
and wake up and us have everything we need
I don't need another family
I just want people to stop being so mean to us
It makes my Daddy cry

now that Ms. Tina
from the agency she for real
I'll tell you how I know
most folk don't look me in the eye
when they speak to me
I mean they do
but really they just lookin' right past me
like I'm a ghost or something
and they just talkin' to the wind

Ms. Tina she looks me in the eye
I can feel her gaze settle on my soul
and when I speak or even when I don't
I can *feel her* listening to me
now that's some real stuff

yeah Ms. Tina
she's not like some other folk
I've even seen her look at Mommy
like Mommy's a real person
Ms. Tina don't know
but after she leaves
Mommy floats around the house
like a queen or something
I like that cause I don't
think most people see Mommy's beauty
does being poor make your beauty
invisible?

Ms. Tina she talks to Daddy
like he's a full grown Man
not a boy
seem like if you're a man like Daddy
in this world
if you stand up all the way they beat you down
and if you crouch down
they smile and pat your back
Daddy wasn't made for that I don't think
but after Ms. Tina leaves I notice Daddy
treats Mommy better
heck
he treats us all better

Ms. Tina she don't know that

it must be hard for Ms. Tina
working with all these families like ours
cause it seems she don't have much support
some days I see her dragging her spirit around
behind her
like it's about to fall off in the dirt and get lost
I wonder if a spirit is like an umbilical cord
wonder if you cut it loose does it shrivel
up and die
hope I never see that happen with Ms. Tina
cause then who would treat us right?

and who's gonna believe in us?
I think it must hurt a soul a whole heap
to have the whole world not believe in 'em
except for one person

wonder if that's what Jesus felt like
when they strung him up on the cross
poor Jesus
he didn't have no Ms. Tina by his side

sometimes I feel like everybody wants to
crucify our family for being the way we are
like we did something wrong by not having
money and making mistakes
don't the people who get to keep their children
make mistakes too?
who's there to scold them?

I remember the time Ms. Tina thought
Ricky and me might have to get put
with another family
or at least in another home
I remember how she sat with us
and made us call all the relatives together
to talk and figure out what to do
I remember how she kept asking
us about our strengths
I thought she meant who had the most muscles
later I realized she meant how did we
deal with our troubles

she kept pushin' at us and pushin' at us
trying to help us help ourselves
eventually we found a way
for Ricky and me to stay in the family
while Mommy got better
Auntie Ruth took us in for a while
but at least my nightmare never came true
they never took my family away

but you know what?
I do believe that if ever Ms. Tina
had to put Ricky and me in another family
I do believe she would pick a good one for us
not any ol' family
I trust Ms. Tina cause
I think we mean something to her
most people when they come in our house
they look around and start frownin'

Ms. Tina
she comes in and her eyes always light up
when she sees us
I don't know if she's just fakin'
far as not likin' what she sees around the house
cause our house   there's not much in it
but at least she cares enough about
our feelings to fake like she's happy to see us
at least she cares enough to act like we mean
something
that's more than we're used to

but Ms. Tina
I think she really does care
if I was the people running the agency
I'd pay her a million dollars
cause that's what she's worth

every time I sleep through the night
and wake up and my nightmare
hasn't come true
that's when I think Ms. Tina
is worth more than gold

when I grow up
I'm going to make something
with my life
just so I can turn around
and thank my Mommy and Daddy
and Ms. Tina
the three big people
who always made me feel like I
was the sunshine
even when the rain was making them wet

Ms. Tina
I know I don't appear to be friendly
on the surface
but that's just cause I'm scared
that if I smile
that's where the pain will sneak in
and come back to visit my heart

she turns the page in her journal
and writes these last words:

my greatest fears:

Mommy dying
Daddy crying
bad things under the bed
somebody taking my family away

p.s.
Ms. Tina:

someday I'm gonna help all the
children just like you do
you ain't just my hero
you're my angel too

you take good care of yourself
I need you to

12-year-old closes her book
emerges from under the sheets
drifts off to sleep
as fireflies mimic the stars
nightmare chased away for
yet another night.

My heart speaks now to you
the one who would serve to toil
on my behalf

I am the child of your daily labor
of your nightly dreams
let me show you something

but wait   I must warn you
what is to be seen lies this way
far within my private garden
in the depths of my treasure chest

come unto me but come unto me true
to venture here you must walk naked
and crying for no cloth must mask your
own frailty
tears must cleanse you well
lest you infect my soul
the very thing you
dare invite yourself beside

I have stories for you
they begin like this:

you see me small and weak
yet my spirit is the ocean
my tide has crept along your shore

I have witnessed your secrets
you bear them alone and shivering

your garden has gone cold
but now is the season in which
you will choose to die or to live

know that this choice is my fate too
as you die or live I die or live with you

our spirits are bound as such
at night you cry out to God
why have you done this to this poor child?

you do not hear God's response:
*what I have done to this poor child I too
have done to you*

my own cry is different in those same nights
I cry *God why have you done this
to the grown ones who toil for me* the child
that they cannot see my Truth?

so you see we are two souls
each crying for the other
forming rivers of tears that
go ungathered

your garden has gone cold
the chill wilts my youthful flower

you cry for me yet your own struggle
steals my sunlight

it is time for you to release your cherry
blossoms and cloud the sky

what then rains down will cleanse your
vision and you will see me true

you will see that as you question
why you do this work
my child heart questions
why you began this work

whose life you serve in bearing this work
when will you at last betray this work
and therefore betray me

you will see that though you have
seen me as poor and pitiable
I am rich and blessed

you see my family roots as rotten
but fail to see that we are a worthy
tree that feeds on rotten ground

your heart loves me but your mind
judges me

you see my chocolate skin as
evidence that I come from something
burnt and broken

so you dream for me of places
bright and distant

my roots are not burnt or barren
only brushed and blemished
yet firm and fertile
my family still has beauty left to forge

you despair about my well fare
I wonder when you will say fare well

stress is a storm sweeping
your valley into dusk
my future in your hands
is your own sunrise

what you touch in me in winter
becomes my gift to you in June

you fear you make no change in
my life
but you forget the darkness
you kept from my life

you suffer a starving pocket
paid light of coin for your work
yet are made rich every moment
of this mission
you look for your payment
in the wrong purse

you spin webs of gold on the fabric
of our childhood futures
but look for fool's gold in false streams

your heart desires approval for the
battles you fight
look to your own echo for that
we create the world in which we live

you wonder how much you can afford
to bleed for me but
your blood is your own salvation

we eat the fruit of seeds we sow
child welfare is a harvest of faith
its true rewards run latent   blossom later
as I grow into the adult who raises
a family like the ones you dream for me

so here we are together
you wish beauty upon me
you *are* the beauty upon me

you have not only come to me
I have come to you
your work is my ministry
your love is my bread
your endurance my breath
your desire my warmth

your pain my hope
your courage my strength
your tears my drink
your nightmares my audience
your faith my shelter

I am your child
but here in my garden you are *my* child
I give birth to your glory
every day that I live

now you see me   don't you?
good   because that is why you are here

this is why we bleed
so that we may send our cherry blossoms
to the sky.

An isolated youth dreams of dignity:

I was Africa once
before the nets and ropes and shackles
and 400-year percolation of spite
that clouded my vision of self

I was Africa and not nearly perfect
but undistorted   rooted   fully human

I was Africa under the palm leaves
dripping with clean rain
civilized more then than
after civilization visited us

I was stronger than the rotting log
teeming with decay
weaker than the granite stone
whitening in the salt of bay

I was the blisters on young hands
learning Old Father's deeply oiled drum

I was sure I was human
I was clear I was beautiful
I was known
I was seen
I was home

I was all that
before I was this

I am Africa still.

She sat down to write this final note
at midnight on her fourteenth birthday
using a carving knife to force
the words directly into the oak table
its flesh gave easily   her courage became words:

I will not fold myself into your genocide
your killing of the ancestors who live
in the marrow of my yearning bones
drumming a song you cannot possess
I am a sun that will not be eclipsed

I will not transcend my heritage
absolutely nothing is wrong with my heritage
I reject your demand that I choose
being human over being my roots
I will be my roots *and* be human
they are indivisible

I will not transcend my truth
become soulless flavorless docility
so that you may avoid reconsidering
the long cathedral of your greatness
you need to transcend your fear of me
transcend your fear of me
your fear of me   fear of me

night was a kind usher
its proud arms steadying her
as for the last time she walked
out the door of the place where
deeds unspeakable were done

she was become.

Maybe it is the full moon
glowing ivory in the indigo sky
that pulls her from her sleep

more likely it is the lifelong hurt
that runs an underground river
through her heart
soaking her insides with an endless
rain of emptiness

the 10-year-old girl peels back her covers
sits up
walks over to the window where
the moon beam illuminates her desk

she sits down there
taking a pen in her hand
sliding a few sheets of her favorite
butterfly stationery close

she begins to write

dear Daddy
this is the 10th year
124th month
3,720th day that I have lived
without you in my life

I know because I count each day
inside my heart

I don't know where you are in this world
so I fantasize
sometimes I think maybe you became an astronaut
got shot up to the moon
maybe you're up there now
the light from your smile shining down on me

oh Daddy
I wish you were here
I'm a big girl now and I'm feeling things
I'm confused

I know you hurt Ma real bad and she hurt you too
but how come I'm the one carrying the blues?
there's a hole where I imagine my peace
should be

I dream of your arms holding me
that's the only time I sleep peacefully
and I know you've done some time
done some crime   slipped and tripped
but how come I'm the punished one?

I don't get to cuddle to your deep voice
I wonder does it sound like thunder?
your eyes are they big like mine?
is your smile wide like mine?
do they too call you chocolate sunshine?

I wish for things
I wish I could go for a walk with you
talk with you
tell you about my 3,720 days

wish you could take me to a Bulls game
or that when I acted in the school play
that you came

wish I could see your face in mine
wish you could tell me about what to do with
the boys at school
'specially with this one fool

wish when they ask *who's your Daddy*
that I could show them you
don't care how you look how you talk
how smart you are what mistakes you've made
just wish I could show them you

they're talkin' about puttin' me in therapy
they can save that money
I don't need no trickery
I need my hollow spot gone
I ain't done wrong
half the music to my song is gone
I need you Daddy to complete my harmony

I'm confused about things
I'm feeling alone

maybe if I have me a baby
maybe if I flirt with that boy Charles
maybe if I wear my skirt real short
maybe if I fight with Ma
maybe if I drink a little   smoke a little
maybe if I scream real loud

you'll hear me all the way out there where you are
you'll come runnin'   find me   see my Truth

my roots are bare and torn from earth
my reflection pond is stirred up muddy
I can't see the reflection of you
the half that completes the whole of me

tomorrow will be day 3,721
if you don't come my tears will run

I remember stories of my birth
Ma gave you 3 weeks to get your act together
social workers gave you 3 months
Daddy now I have to put my foot down

I'm giving you a deadline before I close my heart
I figure I can give you 30   no   300   no   3,000
okay I'll give you 10,000 days but that's it no more

we start counting from
from
whenever you say start

I can't help it I need you in my heart
don't need no super mom no fill-in pops
no shrinks no drugs no grown folk playin' cops

she wrote her final words in bold caps:

I NEED MY DADDY

she got back into bed
full moon kissed her good night.

Hey   over here
look over here
you gotta look hard to see me
I mean   you see the skin of me   the sin of me
but you gotta look *deeper*
I'm not a loser   I'm a keeper

I'm a 15-year-old
packed with fears but feelin' bold
emotions cold   heart laced with gold
I'm a busted up rusted up
gonna dust it up 14-year-old

y'all say I'm troubled tainted dysfunctional
got special needs
but y'all the ones puttin' boulders on my path
you say I'm trippin' but I'm trippin' on your stuff
your anger your fear your prejudice your pain

you say *let's get the boy/girl some intervention*
but what about your therapy?
cause something is making you blind   you can't see me
something is making you deaf   you can't hear me
something is making you scared
you won't truly come near me
something is making you cold   you can't feel me

I act up   you put me on Ritalin
but I'm just dancing
grown folks the ones doin' the fiddlin'
y'all play the wrong song   maybe your song
but not my song
so I try to step correct   keep getting it wrong

for so long I've wanted to wake up in the morning
and hear my song
you say I put on my tunes and tune out the world
I'm not tuning you out   I'm tuning me in
trying to find my frequency
a sound that feels good to me

I'm a 13-year-old switchin' homes
keep putting my stuff in a trash bag
I'm tired of being the trash
I'm not unpacking no more
not unpacking my baggage
my pain my pride my people my trust
see   my attachment tool is starting to rust

you think I'm ungrateful to have a home?
I'm not ungrateful   I'm unsettled

you ever tried to stand still and calm
in an earthquake?
my earth keeps quaking   I'm scared
but you keep wanting me to bond
so I keep faking   but inside I'm quaking

nobody ever asked me what I want in a family
they just moved me like I was a dog
then y'all wonder why I don't act house trained
I may be cracked and bent but I'm not broken

I have my own ideas about family and
what feels good to me
deep in the night if I try real hard
I can find my dreams too
what I want in life

don't want no baby mama baby daddy drama
life already done up and took my mama
never knew my pops
got better relations with parish cops
least they come every time I'm in trouble

ever wonder why I keep getting in trouble?
cause cops is my pops and they spend time with me
my crew on the street   they spend time with me
I'm looking for time not crime
but seems like crime's the way to get
the time so I crimes   drop sin like dimes

I'm that 12-year-old you call violent but
the world is on fire with your anger and screechin'
I'm just the student of what you're teachin'
I'm not preachin' just reachin' to make sense
of this world

don't get me wrong   I have my dreams
I'm trying to build my life
I'm trying to pull fat catfish from my lake so weary
but it seems like all I keep pullin' is pollution
from my water so dreary
I'm tryin' to find the sunshine
life keeps giving me rain

you say pray   have faith good things will come today
it's hard to pray when my nightmares
keep breakin' in on my day

but yesterday I had me a vision
a way to turn my life around

I'm gonna take all the pain
packed away in my chest
release it to the sky   give it a rest

I'm gonna use it to show my baby sister
how much I've missed her
see   Pops tried to shoot my mama
missed her   took out my sister
now my heart's a blister
cause Lord I've missed her

but now I'm gonna turn my pain into paint
and paint me a rainbow
show the young ones which way to walk
which way not to go

I'm gonna be a teacher a preacher a healer a reacher
I'm gonna shine my light   shine it real bright
you know why?
cause that way maybe you'll have to see me

you'll see I'm a 12 14 16 18-year-old
a little bruised   a whole lot bold
so don't pity me   look down at me
frown at me   grieve me
best believe me
I'm gonna shed my skin and shake my sin
I'm gonna *make you see me.*

Young brothers of every skin
fronting hard and feeling tender
heads nodding to the rhythm
skin bakin' to browns blacks
and reds
in the sunlight reflected
off unforgiving concrete
steps

sayin *amen* and *that's all right*
this could be church
they could be congregation
this could be a preacher
they listen to
as he feeds them his latest
sermon

except this is not church

in the penitentiary
during fleeting yard time
serving for hard crime
they with their pent up stories
pushing the peddles that release
their feet
provide the beat

he
who could be a preacher
is a juvenile inmate
intimates with his brothers
provides the heat

they tap
he raps:

I've got tats on my tri's
and yokes on my bi's
cold in my heart kicks the lights
peeps your lies

I'm pacing like a caged cougar
on the yard
liftin plates and pressin hard

hollerin at my dreams
between the icy bars

dreams are flying away
and out of reach

I'm the bloated fish
washed up on the beach

all these seagulls
pickin at my flesh
wanna breathe the good air
can't get none fresh

carrying my water
in a pot made of mesh

aching for my daughter
cause I sold her to the slaughter
and it bought her

now I'm spilling the last
of my salty water

shootin jumpers on the gray
sun blastin brothers as we play
only game that got us
look where all this ballin brought us

can't twitch a muscle
without a tussle from the warden
and his system hustle

stepping proper for the Man
feeling like the lowest
and not a man

all these *swolled up* brothers
with shrunken brains
done washed their keys
right down the drains

laughin at the suits
but now who's wearing
prison regs
matching jumpers
and matching grills
passing balloons
powdered from the pills

passing lifetimes making deals
never getting out
never getting over

signing on the bottom line
never reading the finer print
contracts got us buzzing
keep us loaded for killing cousins
dozens die for every six
who see the light

fleets of fireflies
blinded by the night

system shackles on the
left foot

mental shackles on the
right

shuffling around the crowded cage
family reunion of the slaves

guess we need to bump up
the glory music louder
before we hear the drums
that make us prouder

takes a slick beat
to kick this slickness
400 trips around this sickness

gotta be the one to slip this track
gotta get my quickness back

gotta flip the switch
and 'scape this yard
trying hard but hatred's trying harder

gotta pawn my fears
to make this final barter

long as this nation denies its madness
it's all on me to climb
the purple mountains majesty

can't be no worse
than dying in the desert
of my thirst
and walking ghostly
on the yard

baby daughter
I'm coming for ya
tell all the ones
who wanna keep you
from your daddy
they can't touch the golden bridge
God has built between us

all the taint aint enough
to split us
from the heaven
that will admit us
as a baby and her father

I'm going deep inside the slaughter
mending fences in my heart

a wiser brother schooled me
said greatness lives within
I'm signing no more dotted lines
I already own all a mines

I don't need the Man's release
just daily praying from humble knees

no more signing hatred's lease
I own my own piece
I own my peace

If you can't feel me
get up off my land
I'm cleaning up all my
soiled sand

I'm sweeping sacred
spirit from the corners
of my being
I once was frightful blind
but now I'm steady seeing

I once did this gig as child
now I'm going manhood
and bowing down
to lift me up

no more slavin'
on the plantation
of my mind

I'm setting my mentality
ten times past free

I own my own light
I own my truth
I own my peace

Peace.

The dream was crazy

he was 18 and standing before a judge
courtroom was packed with social workers
lawmakers politicians police probation officers
juvee-heads teachers preachers lawyers therapists
and every foster family he ever had

judge looked down at him and said:

here you stand in judgment
of your *e-mancipation*
tell the court why you believe
you are prepared to become
a productive member of society

young man took himself a swallow
stood tall and let his truth be heard:

your honor
I started out this life as a hummingbird
just looking for a place to land and
for whatever reason
life kept switching up my nest

I did my best to go with the flow
from this nest to that nest
after a while my wings needed rest
I decided that from now on
I'm gonna flex my X

judge frowned   looking down and said
what do you mean flex your X?

young man replied
X is that thing you pick up every time
a family throws you down

it's that hunger that burns inside
to feel like you belong

it's the way you learn to see past lies
and find the truth

it's the beauty born of a private pact
to prove yourself

y'all see us as nothing more than
train wrecks and rejects
full of missteps and defects
but we're a new nation
we're about to flex our pecs

every day until we *age out* of your system
we're building dreams inside
age-ing *into* our life mission
foster care is a journey of attrition and ambition
I wouldn't even be alive at 18
if I hadn't lit my own ignition

sometimes I doubt myself
and my fear chases me
with claws and teeth like T-Rex
but then I remember I was *given* this life
to shape me into something special

someone who cares about other people's pain
and situations in life

foster care taught me not to give love pecks
when people need compassion
and their due respects

holding back our love is what wrecks
the whole human complex

see X is that factor inside picked up from
the extraordinary foster care ride
it's about learning how to overcome the hex
and make it your reflex to thrive
that's how come I'm extraordinary
and I'm still alive

y'all in this courtroom can stop craning your necks
we're not rejects with defects
we're like X-Men
we've got super-powered reflex

we've been called mutant and outcast
but we learned what makes each of us special
our life in foster care is one of those things
now when life shines its light through our X
that light reflects on objects lying in our path
we have new vision

we step over   we step forward   we rise

we've got a passion y'all can never know
a passion to set the world straight
a passion to grow

we've got stories to tell and gifts to give
we dare to live our lives
in super-powered 3-D
not like super-ficial cartoons on TV
we're fully human and full of destiny

so when they treat us like suspects
we just flex our X
when they call us derelicts
we stand tall and represent our reality
like Memorex
then we use our truth in steps
to rise up over the mountain
and reach our apex
we keep coming up aces
no matter the decks

when you run your checks on your rolodex
you'll find us listed under heroes and she-roes
because we survived then thrived
so with all due respects judge sir
I'm not emancipating or aging out
I'm stepping in   stepping up
I'm about to change the game

to all my people in foster care
when life gives you mess
don't stress
just FLEX YOUR X!

The legislator:

We need to remove barriers to loving homes

The parent:

I love all my children the same

The child filled with old soul:

We do not honor the One Spirit
of which we are composed
by pretending sameness
but by watering the soil
of our many nations
and feeding that
garden to the

seven
generations
to come

This is Love.

A child's heart to heart with *the system*:

gracefully I ask   did you look for my father
under that rock
for my uncle under that tree

did you tear up the city
to find my cousin
who might have carried me?

what of my auntie
who used to kiss and cuddle me?

when was it that you met
each of my family
since you have determined that
none in my family are worthy of me?

why does the
sterility of *normalcy*
mean more than
the richness inside
our family poverty?

why do you value
the norms you bleed
over the things I need?

I like costumes and masks
but not on the ones charged
with the task of raising me

from them I need
nakedness and honesty
I need the courage of frailty
I need to understand
why they keep tripping on me

you say my family had no treasures
you never opened the chest

you see no beauty in my people
because you cannot *see* my people
you see only ghosts
clothed in the sheets
of ideas you have been taught

how can you assume people
who scorn what I come from
can make me feel loved?

a recipe for self-hatred
lives in your philosophy

here is what I pray
that you don't paint
these challenging words
as troubled or whatever
adjective-agent used to wash
truth down the drain

I pray that you find
dignity breaking through my pain

can you find a reason
to look deeper at your motives
your method   your mind?

you may discover that
I am worth more than a contract
that soothes a budget line

some people pay for a child
but the child is who gets billed
for lack of consideration
of the difference between
child spirit filled
and
child spirit killed

with all due respect
to the complex
challenge of placing me

I will ask one more time
did you tear up this world
to find
blood kin or otherwise
the ones who truly
should be mine?

speak truth to me
and we will have a garden
where our imperfections sow
the seeds that grow
to beautiful.

Heart to heart continues . . .

Next time devoted one   could you
find it in your heart
to ask the families who
just wanted to give a child a better life
to list the things they thought
would make my life better

could you ask them to name
the ways they fear me
fear my people
fear my fear

how they plan to help me know myself
how can they help me dry my tear?

how if they don't know
what I've lost
can they help me find it again?

do they believe that my past
is part of my better life?

are my traditions part
of my better life?

are my old friends
part of my better life?

can my dreams be part
of my better life?

how about my memories
of what felt good to me?

how about my fitting in?
not sticking out?
having not to shout
to be heard from inside?

I weigh what was
against what is
a thousand times a day

I'm not sure what
better means in your mind
but I have a feeling
some of my *better* I've left behind

do you mind?

some of my better
is found in today
and what looks to be coming

do you think a singer
would be better if she
had to choose between
notes of her humming
or a drummer between
beats of his drumming?

I am asking for your help here
does better start where trouble ends
or do new troubles mean
that now better begins?

can I miss what I had
and be loved in the present?

can I live in the future
to manage the ghosts of my past?

and if I miss my family
and my school can't be family
and my teams can't be family
and my friends   teachers   coaches
neighbors   world can't be family

and if my family can't be family

can I at least choose
in my heart
who gets to be
family to me?

I know I cannot control
the weather or whether
tough times come my way
I am reminded of this
every moment of day

but can I at least choose
who to let in my heart?

can I choose?

I'm not sure what better is
but I believe
a choice is a start.

It was a tea party with her favorite doll
beneath the cooling pines
in her lemon summer dress
something on her heart to confess
to her porcelain friend:

You are that gentle butterfly   and I
I that hand that must remain
a soft and freeing place to land

the butterfly I have spoken of
so often in the past
thinking it was I pleading for
a hand that did not grasp or
smother my fragile light

the butterfly I sought beneath
my bed at night
and on the perches of flowers
in my dreams
and ran to barefoot across
wet morning grass
when sun was new
that butterfly was not I
she was you

you are that gentle butterfly   and I
I must remain a good and safe
landing place

I will do this for you

butterfly
and I.

The letter was written on sun bleached
paper the frail consistency of old skin
tucked in her favorite journal where
her child   as of yesterday a college student
and far away from

home

knew she would find it

she sat on her auburn couch
near the window in morning's
eager light
and read
a starburst of revelation
a bundling of years of the unsaid
a kindling for new love

she had never encountered
her baby's voice in this
inspired persona

this is what her baby's courage said:

There is no simplicity in relationship, only moments ripe
with potential for joy and pain. Both sensations may bring
us growth. This is a truth as relevant for parent as for
progeny. I believe a child is a spirit with the strength to
withstand storms on the way toward fulfilling life
purpose, but is also blessed with a delicateness of
sensitivity and intense feeling.

What to us in our more tenured years are bland expanses of emotions in reaction to life are vibrant explosions of waterfall and lava to a child in the midst of raw wonder. Each moment in the experience of family, for a child carries treasure chests of emotion we can only strive to imagine from our grownup vantage point.

I as an adopted child need things most particular from you. Love, which you may consider as the crowning of my provisions, is, though precious, only the baseline of my sustenance. I am *of Life*, come to you, and by nature I am a social being. I develop myself through my relationship to and experience with other human beings, and with Life itself.

Because of this I need these basic human requirements, which should be written up as human rights, and exercised as our human salvation: I need to feel a sense of connection to you. I need to know that you go beyond the quick and easy step of loving and into the challenging and rich process of respecting all that I am, and may come to be, even to the extent that my truth may discomfort you. I need you to address me with truth and not deception-as-a-means-of-protection.

I need you to understand that my identity, self-esteem, and ability to nourish myself stem from the health of your identity, self-esteem, and ability to nourish yourself. I need that you not exercise impulses borne of your own insecurities as you raise me, but that you exercise those impulses in other spaces. So that I may receive from you parenting derived of a mentor's wisdom—you have come before me on this path.

I need that you spend time working on your understanding of why you adopted me. To communicate, not only early on and initially, but also enduringly, and in many ways why you chose *this particular manner of embracing particular me.* Do not tell me why you wanted *a* child, but why you want and love *this* child—me.

Do not expect a child to easily accept her arrival through adoption as being as natural and unquestionable as that through birth; our natural propensity in life is to ask why. Tell me why the sky is blue and tell me why I am a part of you.

Just as all children need constant reminders of their parent's love, I need consistent validation of *the goodness of my distinctiveness from you.* Not direct redundancy, but varied portrayal of the values you claim to have as reason for wanting me. Let it show up not only in direct conversation, but also in the way you live; the way you relate to certain other people and places and events. Let your living be your proof.

If you do not provide me this, I will answer such questions about my place in your world and this world myself, and I will answer from the insecurity of my searching. If you do not want society and its strangers to provide my answers, then you be my messenger. Use honesty, and if you are not sure about a thing, then use that opportunity to show me what it means to be human: Tell me that you do not know, but will invest in coming to know. If I know that you have made an effort in regard to an aspect of *Me*, even if it is not directly an aspect of *You*, then I will later in my life know something more of what it means to be *We*.

I need that you remind yourself which of the two of us is the priority when it comes to sacrifice of the ego or comfort. I am tender. You are life-tested. I need you to go about this work with the diligence and frequency that you might give to your own education, work, passions, and other relationships. And then give more. I need you to take the weight of perfection expectations off your shoulders, so that you can stand taller and take deeper breaths as you raise me with a devoted imperfection. I will remember not your imperfection, but your perfect commitment to my entirety. I need you to reflect, reckon, heal, and grow so that you can shepherd me to my same.

I need for culture to become a reality in your consciousness, like the weather is now, so that you respond to its realities within our family, within yourself, and within me. I need those responses to be humble and fluid as they relate to how you have been socialized through your own cultural experiences.

What you believe and expect for others (especially family) to respect, may not be what I come to believe and need for others (especially you my family) to respect. I need you to know that my life is to be lived toward the purpose of my blossom. If you have not already reached your blossom, humbling yourself to the integrity, validity, and dignity of my spirit may fertilize your own blossom.

I need for you to not be afraid of me. What sounds absurd is truly at the core of many family relationships. It is the feeling of threat to our sense of validity and worth that flames us toward jealousy, resentment, defensiveness, control, a deaf ear, a blind eye, spite, and power-tripping in our way of relating to a loved one.

I need for you to accept that the ideas, values, and people that I identify myself with as I grow will surely be influenced by you, but that they will not ultimately be dictated by you. I will remember forever your guiding arms and words, but will spill tears throughout my years in thanks for the freedom that you allowed my spirit, which is by nature a force of freedom.

I need for you to not magnify or obsess over my adoptive circumstance, nor my ethnic or other distinctive character. I need for you equally to not ignore, deny, or avoid the same things about me. My characteristics and circumstance are not cartoons to be exaggerated or gawked over, nor are they meant for invisibility or to become *something the family doesn't talk about*. But neither am I tragic-drama. Be light with yourself in discovering me. I believe that balance is the key. My truth is like your personality: it is a thing that simply is. And when it is not attended to, appreciated, or respected, not only do I not feel good, but also I am diminished. You who claim to Love me are then tethered to that smothering of the flame, and we both grow cold.

Please do not be misled by the surface decorations of ease and discomfort, for what comes easy to you in dealing with my needs may truly be a spoonful of bad medicine for both of us. And what comes through discomfort as you struggle to do right by me may be the most loving potion you may offer.

I need you to not feel threatened by the people and experiences I have descended from in body and spirit, through the generations of time. Rather you should relate to these roots of mine as jewels in the treasure chest you acquired in your initial embrace of me. These jewels can be your support as you raise me, so please do not through insecurity and fear try to separate me from what I have come from, of what I am a part. These things, more so than any nation or manmade thing, are indivisible, and you will only have succeeded in causing disruption within me. You need me to be whole, so that we as a family can be whole. And my intimacy with people and culture not of you and yours is in fact a central ingredient in my intimacy with you and yours.

I need urgently and critically that you find the motivation, reason, courage, and strength to plunder the holds of your soul for the prejudice that we all surely carry, and spend some time with those energies; especially as they relate to social categories into which this world might place me. For, how can you honestly carry prejudice in your heart toward what is a part of me? No manner of costume, makeup, or mask that you may adorn to disguise yourself from me would be powerful enough to stay your prejudices from me. In the end you would only betray yourself in single, forever lasting words, actions, and energy. And I would always have to carry that painful contradiction of love living in the place where I should not be confused—in my family.

I am child and so I need. I need. I need. I need. But a secret I can share with you is this: What I need, you also need. I am complex but ever so simple, just as you are. Look for me, truly look for me with sincerity, and you will know what is best for me. I believe in you, in what you have come from, and where you are going. Believe the same of me, and when I grow, whatever pain I may have come through, I will look back upon my life beside you with thankfulness because you raised me with a humble imperfection, and set me free. I drink from you. I find comfort beside you. I find myself in you.

You are my reflection pond.

Calm the water's surface for my looking.

The student was given a choice
of subjects for the oral presentation
chose to speak on Nature:

The nature of my roots
is not as decisive
in my life as is the nature
of the earth come to bind with me

earth of relations feed me
water me   pollute me   poison me
heal me   strengthen me hold me
fail me   become me   shape me

will you spit me out
soil of my present day?
or take me in
which requires you mold
yourself intimately
around the shape of my soul

teacher of this moment
you are all the light
I have been given for
this stretch of road

shine on me
light my path before me
reveal what lurks around me
in pregnant shadows

but I beg of you   *be the light*
be the good earth   a steady bed
the stronger soil   a richer spot
in fallow ground

come be my earth

my roots are made to respond
to ground that feeds them

stroke my ends so bravely
and we shall make amends
I will send my shoots deeper *deeper*

I will become such a tree
quite the vine
accomplished flower
a cause enough for planting

I make good seed
just wrap me in your courageous
soil poised to learn

find my worth   dirty my husk of seed
wet the shell   soak my flesh
coax my   downward sprout

my upward is pulled by Sun Above
downward thrust though
is a rooting *must*
a fingering through
thick and buried mud

find my worth   bring on my suckle
be my good   and courageous earth.

Another move   another starting over

a leaf flutters
a heart joins the dance
a child begs the world:

I have met the bitter wind
abrupt end to habit's shelter

kneel with me now
as the mud grows deep and cold
for I do not know the rate
of my descent
nor whether the ground line
shall rise to consume me

pray thee that I might
be buried but to become a seed
and sprout again
green and not broken thusly
yearning again
to pierce the crust
and wave with confidence
beneath the sky of a rain retreated

this life
this piercing life
sweeps us low
the plowing
raises us high
the harvest

what majestic winds we bear
what brunt of storm
before the weeping calm
that ushers in new light
and leaves us

gasping spent
gaping open
bridled bound

ears to soil
anticipating
next unanticipated
unyielding sound

wading into waters unknown
begins with a shifting in the heart
long before movement finds our legs

inertia is a beauty we serenade
until it swells and fills our cup
scales down its castle wall
to settle within us
the peasant dreaming
of what life is
beyond the moment
whose ground we have trodden
the garden whose soil we have leached
the time whose circles
we have worn bare

move
we say
to our own stillness
it does

move

we are brave now
leaves turn
even as buds stir within
the branch
eager for showy spring

we will meet that warm
season at its birth
for now we are motion
as all things living should be

smile creases the face
of our desire

even as we splash
the puddles of change
into clouds of anxiety
we are coming clean

even as we strain to
un-become this weary note
we are learning a new song

a song first sung
by a shifting in the heart.

The teacher was moved to tears
as she read the story turned in
for her seventh-grade class
by a boy whose turbulent life
could not dim his promise:

A MAN led his small boy down the path toward home. On the way they passed a wheat field where an older man toiled in the heat. The elder was revered in the community as someone who had a deft touch for bringing peace to local conflicts, and for soothing suffering hearts. The father cleared his throat and called out, Son, say hello to this gentleman. He is a great man.

The elder replied, Thank you for your kind words. However I fear you surpass reality with your view of me.

But you are such a wise man, the father replied. You seem to see things others do not. It is as though you have access to a world beyond this one.

No, the elder offered. I am not a wise man. My intellect is simple and my thoughts hard to come by, I do believe. I am simply a man who uses his pain well.

This brought wonder across the father's face. What do you mean you use your pain well?

The elder stood up, straightened his spine, and looked the father in the eye with a gentle gaze. A farmer of course cares about his crops, yes?

Yes, of course.

Well, then, what farmer would use only the sunlight that comes to his field but avoid using the rain water that falls, keeping it from his growing harvest?

None, of course.

Yes. None, of course. Then why do you feel that so many souls use only the sunlight of life but run away from the rain of life? You see, the sunlight of life is those pleasant moments and experiences that bring us easy joy and laughter. We don't think twice about rolling around in that hay, celebrating it, making it a part of our personal and family heritage. Those pleasant emotions become the food of our storytelling feast. We reflect on those feelings. Because they feel good to us, we enjoy exploring those feelings for their deeper meaning. You could say that most of us use our happiness well.

I see, said the father, holding his young son by the shoulders, fast at attention. Please continue.

Unfortunately, too many of us run away from the rain of life. The rain of life is the pain of life: The deeply hurtful and difficult feelings that come from our unpleasant experiences. The rain of life is the wounded-ness that comes to us as an unavoidable daily dose. It is part of the parcel of being alive. But we have been taught to take the pain of life as a negative thing, as a thing to avoid at all costs. This is neither accurate nor realistic.

The pain of life is not negative; it is difficult. There is a difference. A negative thing has no potential other than destruction and harm. A difficult thing may be unpleasant yet its greatest potential is when it is used for something productive and positive.

We cannot ultimately avoid pain. It is sewn into the moments of our being. The rain that falls from the sky may leave us soaked and cold and wishing for the sun, but that very rain is feeding our crop; satisfying our harvest; it brings us just as much chance for good things to happen as does the sun. And yet we run away.

With the pain of life, we talk about how the past is the past; and it's important to move on; to not dwell in darkness and so forth. We have constructed an entire language for our children that teaches them quite stupendously to treat the pain of life as insurmountably negative and something to flee desperately.

The truth is just the opposite. We must teach our children that they may enter straight into their pain; confront it honestly; and with the proper tools they can nurture that pain into some of the most powerful personal characteristics a soul may carry.

Most of all among these is compassion: The capacity and habit of wishing for others that they do not suffer. From a compassionate heart an amazing river may flow forth from any of us. A river born of the work we have done with our pain; a river that is often misinterpreted, as mine is, as wisdom or unearthly insight.

A long moment of silence. Then the father spoke: You have humbled me and opened me all at once. I believe I hear you saying that most of us waste fully one half of what life brings us. That simply by making use of the daily grace of pain, just as we make use of the daily grace of joy, we can see ourselves and each other much more clearly.

The elder's creased face smoothed into a smile. I could not have put it more *wisely* myself. Why not use what we are given? Life gives us joy and pain, and nature is in harmony with this truth by offering the world sunshine and rain. Both bring growth and fruit to the crop of souls. So instead of leaving our pain to rot and fester in the internal bins we construct with our fear, I say sit down with it and learn to know it, for there is sour yeast in even the sweetest of breads.

The father turned his son down the path. Goodbye, Sir, and thank you for this lesson. I see in the clouds that the rain soon comes. I'm going to get my son home.

So that you can avoid the rain?

No, Sir. So that we can gather the rest of the family and go stand out in the rain!

The elder clapped with vigor and grinned his hearty satisfaction. Go, my children. Go and use your pain well, and reap the harvest of a beautiful life!

Good night   teddy bear
are you feeling lonely?

tonight I'm going to tell you a story
and sing you a song
so you can smile while you sleep
and tomorrow we'll spend the whole
day just listening to each other

I know that makes us both feel better

okay . . .

Uncle Samuel told me once that people spend their lives acting foolish because they think who they are ends where their bodies ends. He said if we could see ourselves as we truly are, as music flowing into each other, we would know that we can't treat each other bad because the whole world is just like a spider's web, and each of us is only a strand in that web.

He said a body don't mean nothing, but that it's the song in the body that counts. The song tells us what we're doing here, and lets us find out what we mean to each other by singing our song and listening to everyone else's song. He said our song is our spirit, and when we call out with it, it bounces off of everything, even the sky, and comes back to us. That lets us know where we are in the world and where we need to be.

I guess that makes our song the thing that allows us to know who we are and where we came from. Because if we can hear our own song, I mean listen real close like, then we can know where it came from, who gave it to us, and where we need to go with it.

Uncle Samuel says people get lost because somehow along the way on their road things happened to separate them from their song, or to make their song become quiet. Like with slavery or poverty or homelessness. Or when somebody treats us bad, or when there is nobody around who understands our song in the first place. Or just when someone tries to choose our song for us.

Here is a song that I have for you:

> Oh my teddy
> you're my best friend
>
> you listen to me
> even when
>
> I say the same things
> over again
>
> about my heart
> and now and then
>
> about the dreams
> I carry here
>
> to one day cry
> a silver tear

and wrap it in
a cloth of love

and bring it
to my mother dear

so she can
plant it in her garden

and it will grow
from silver tear

to a vine of roses
and mother dear

can finally mend
her longing heart

and see how she
and her baby child

are not so far apart
indeed

see distance can be
made less hard

when we imagine
the bridge of love

that spans all miles
and never fails to hold

even when all else
grows cold

and evaporates
like summer snow

I'm a child
but this I know

spirit is a body
without end

and what was lost
will come again

at least in love
if not in flesh

and so I smile
in my rest

I know mother
mother dear

is not gone
but warm and near

oh my teddy
you're my best friend

you listen to me
even when . . . .

and now I kiss you
to your sleep

teddy teddy
you're my
best   friend.

I am your child
I am a jazz note
play me

I am silence
make music with me

this time I'll be the saxophone reed
purse your lips
kiss me so I soften and bend
to your breath

kiss me

this time I'll be the fingers
you be the keys
when I stroke your notes
surrender to me   to me

our home is an orchestra pit
an opera house
the walls are soaked with your song
now let's play mine too

I want to *hear* me when I wake
in the morning
I want the sun to rise and warm me
I want the wind to race through
the house and splash over me
I want you to greet me with a
freestyle harmony
you play the base line
me I'll do the treble cleft

make my breakfast eggs taste
like hallelujah in my mouth
seasoned with your sweetness
from this spicy Cajun South

I'll put on my clothes for school
but I'll still be cold because
my nightmares keep leaving a chill

so drape me in melody:
the stories from your child days
wrap me in your chorus line:
blended passions that fill your heart

and here's a start:
praise me

even as you hold me
scold me mold me lift me
pray for me lead me show me . . .
praise me

cause when I   leave your house
our house   I hear music   strange fruit
I hear songs   sung wrong
I hear flat notes   sharp tones
broken melodies   hate stained piano keys
I hear people   in the street
at school and   on TV
singing *at* me   not to me   with me
but at me   through me

they blue me   scare me
doubt me   shoo me   they take me
break me   betray me   scorn me
pity me   but never   see me

they string me   not musically
but up a tree   where they noose me
then kick out   the base beneath my feet
they loose me   I swing loosely

I like drawing and sports and movies
they paint me bland and flawed
and . . . see . . . I groove ease-y
I groove easy

you can plow my field
hoe my soil
make valley where I toil
hurt me with a single raindrop
cause my ground is baked hard and cracked

I'm not broken
not a foster plaything token
my fate just got to smokin'
now I'm hard but hardly broken

some days I catch God's glory rays
feel like slammin' down crawfish étouffées

other times I'm suckin'
limes and feeling sour
cause grown folks toss me like a hand grenade
scared of me but *they* got all the power

some days I'm grinnin' like Satchmo
or scowling like Miles

maybe I'm bluesy like Louisi-ana in the rain
or just hanging in the mist
with brother John Coltrane

what I'm sayin' is
I'm not the spot   I'm not the stain
I'm that tune that takes you
dances in your brain

find my pain my joy my purpose my song
sing me hold me pray me

scold me make bold me hear me say me
Luther sang it
make this house a home
no more wander no more roam

you love me? good   now see me
you can't be me but believe me
I need you to release me so *I* can be me

so sing me song me right me
cause this world done wrong me

tell me why you think I am the Beauty
cause life tells me I am the Beast

leave love letters in my bed
scatter them like rose petals through the house
I'll find them read them
come to love myself

I am your child
I am a jazz note

Play me.

The young man
displaced from his homeland
and family and now a mentor
delivers his closing
Achievement Ceremony address
to the audience
younger people completing
a rites of passage program
for refugees and migrant
souls no longer judged
in the context of their
natural cultural beauty

for they live in a world
that does not know them

therefore they have had
to retreat into the trees
among those who care
so they might rediscover their light

therefore they are here
to hear:

You were born beautiful. You have always belonged. All
that is required of your life is for you to spend it
discovering your beauty and realizing that *to which* you
belong. You have an eternal, all-powerful song. If you find
it, sing it, you can't go wrong.

Remember who you are. A descendant should have a memory of that from which she descends. Without this memory she is not whole. She is lost inside the illusion that her life is an individual journey, a solitary foray. Inside your heart live many ancestors. They will be strong and brave for you.

Congratulations from the place in my heart where hope is found, for your achievements of graduation and transition. Your greatest achievement is not a grade or a diploma. It is the way in which you have shaped your character. How you treat yourself and others will define your life.

I have all faith in you. I pray that you always have the will to shine your light. This world needs your illumination! Be a lantern. Be the way home for a child somewhere.

A young friend once shared with me the name she gave herself. She wrote it in music. Now I write it into you. Your name is . . .

eternal cause
rain of ages
eager vine
brave sojourn
daily author
tango sun
leaping heart
deep seer
waking tide

your name is . . . *Beautiful* . . . .

INDEX OF FIRST LINES

It was a tea party with her favorite doll, 144
February 9, 1999.

The letter was written on sun bleached, 145
October 5, 1998.

The student was given a choice, 151
January 20, 2008.

Another move another starting over, 153
This poem is a combination of three separate poems, written
April 30, 2000, October 6, 2003, and October 10, 2003.

The teacher was moved to tears, 156
March 9, 2006.

Good night teddy bear, 160
October 5, 1998.

I am your child, 164
Written and recited as part of a keynote for the Louisiana
Department of Social Services, Office of Community Services,
New Orleans Region, Foster & Adoptive Parent Appreciation
Luncheon, New Orleans, LA. May 28, 2004.

The young man, 168
May 18, 2007.

Jaiya John lives in Silver Spring, Maryland. He is blessed with the beauty of his daughter and serves his life mission through writing, speaking, and mentoring. He is the founder and executive director of Soul Water Rising, a human relations mission stirring the soul to remember itself. Jaiya gives truest thanks to the following:

R. Eric Stone created the cover design for *Beautiful* and the Soul Water Rising logo. He is a scenic designer and educator in theatre, and a graphic designer. www.rericstone.com.

Jacqueline V. Richmond, Charlene R. Maxwell, and **Kent W. Mortensen** served as the editorial team for *Beautiful*.

Other Books by Jaiya John

To learn more about this and other books by Jaiya John, to order discounted bulk quantities, or to learn about Soul Water Rising's global human relations work, please visit us at: www.soulwater.org.

WWW.SOULWATER.ORG
WWW.JAIYAJOHN.COM

Printed in the United States
221085BV00001B/14/P

9 780971 330832